Bergson

Bergson

Leszek Kolakowski

ST. AUGUSTINE'S PRESS
South Bend, Indiana

Manufactured in the United States of America.

2 3 4 5   23 22 21 20 19 18 17

Library of Congress Cataloging in Publication Data
Kolakowski, Leszek.
Bergson / Leszek Kolakowski.
p. cm.
Originally published: Oxford; New York: Oxford
University Press. 1985, in series: Past masters.
Includes bibliographical references and index.
ISBN: 978-1-890318-11-6 (alk. paper)
Bergson, Henri, 1859–1941. I. Title.
B2430.B43 K64 2000
194 – dc21   00-062609

∞ *The paper used in this publication meets the minimum requirements*
of the American National Standard for Information Science –
Permanence of Paper for Printed Materials. ANSI Z39-1984

ST. AUGUSTINE'S PRESS
www.staugustine.net

Contents

Abbreviations

References in the text are given by an abbreviation of the title, followed by a volume reference (where relevant) and a page reference. Unless otherwise indicated below, these page references are to the standard edition of Bergson's works, *Oeuvres*, ed. André Robinet (Presses Universitaires de France, 1970).

C   *L'Évolution créatrice* (Creative Evolution)

E   *Essai sur les données immédiates de la conscience* (Essay on the Immediate Data of Consciousness)

M   *Matière et mémoire* (Matter and Memory)

R   *Le Rire* (Laughter)

S   *L'Énergie spirituelle* (Mind-energy)

T   *Les Deux Sources de la morale et de la religion* (The Two Sources of Morality and Religion)

W   *Écrits et paroles*, ed. R.-M. Mossé-Bastide (3 vols, Presses Universitaires de France, 1957–9)

Quotations are in my own translation.

Main dates in Bergson's life

The life of Henri Bergson was academic and, on the face of it, uneventful. He was born in Paris on 18 October 1859. His father, a Polish Jew, was a music teacher and a composer, his mother a Jewess from the north of England; thanks to her Bergson was familiar with the English tongue from his childhood. After graduating from high school (the Lycée Condorcet), Bergson was admitted in 1878 to the École Normale: Jean Jaurès entered the school in the same year, Durkheim a year earlier. After graduation in 1881, Bergson was appointed Professor of Philosophy in a *lycée*, first in Angers, and in 1883 in Clermont-Ferrand. He moved back to Paris in 1888 and taught successively in three *lycées*, the longest time in the Lycée Henri IV (1890–8). In 1898 he was appointed Maître de Conférence (the rough equivalent of a Reader in a British university) at the École Normale. By then his first work, *Essai sur les données immédiates de la conscience*, which was his doctoral thesis, appeared along with the Latin thesis, *Quid Aristoteles de loco senserit* (1889), as well as *Matière et mémoire* (1896). He applied twice (in 1894 and 1898) for a post at the Sorbonne; Durkheim is said to have been instrumental in the failure of his application.

In 1891 Bergson married Louise Neuberger; they had one daughter, born deaf, who was to become a painter.

Bergson was awarded a Chair at the Collège de France in 1900 and, the following year, elected member of the Académie des Sciences Morales et Politiques. In 1900 he published *Le Rire* and in 1907 *L'Évolution creátrice*, a work which soon became immensely popular and established his world reputation. He did not travel much, but in 1911 he delivered lectures in Oxford and Birmingham and in 1913 in New York.

In 1914 Bergson's major works were put on the Index of prohibited books by the Holy Office; Jacques Maritain is said to have been active in causing this move, the obvious reason for which was Bergson's great popularity among the advocates of Catholic modernism. In the same year he was elected to the Académie Française.

During the war Bergson occasionally published short essays on current topics and in February 1917 made a diplomatic voyage to the United States. His mission was to convince the Administration and the President that America should join the war against the central powers. To what extent his effort influenced events is difficult to assess. After the war he was elected first President of the Commission Internationale de Coopération Intellectuelle. He resigned in 1925.

In 1919 *L'Énergie spirituelle* appeared; it was a collection of essays dealing mainly with the mind–body problem, written between 1900 and 1914. His next work, *Dureé et simultanéité*, appeared in 1922; this was a discussion with Einstein on the meaning and consequences of the theory of relativity.

In 1927 Bergson was awarded the Nobel Prize for Literature. His last major work, *Deux sources de la morale et de la religion*, was published in 1932, followed two years later by *La Pensée et le mouvant*, a collection of essays going back to 1903; it included, however, two texts never published before.

In 1937 Bergson wrote his last will, in which he says that he would receive baptism in the Catholic Church were it not for the growth of anti-Semitism: he wants to remain among the persecuted. At the same time he formally forbids the publication of any of his manuscripts, letters, or notes.

On 3 January 1941 Bergson died in occupied Paris from pneumonia contracted after standing for many hours in a queue to be registered as a Jew.

1 Beyond science

Bergson's central idea

When we look at Bergson's position – or rather lack of position – in today's intellectual life, we find it hard to imagine that some decades ago he was not just a famous thinker and writer; in the eyes of Europe's educated public he was clearly *the* philosopher, the intellectual spokesman *par excellence* of the era. His popularity reached its peak in the last years before the First World War, especially after the publication of *Creative Evolution* (1907), but his influence was widely felt all over Europe in the twenties and thirties only to vanish almost completely after the Second World War. At their peak, his prestige and impact could only be compared to the vogue Sartre enjoyed in the late forties and early fifties. Bergson's lectures in the Collège de France were weekly social events attended by a good many of the Parisian élite; by the First World War all his major works had been published in English, German, Polish, and Russian, and some of them had appeared in many other languages. The French literary public was fed with many articles and books either extolling the new philosophy or passionately attacking it. In 1914 the Holy Office put his works on the Index of prohibited books, a measure which was very rarely applied to non-Catholic writers and which itself proved how formidable Bergson's influence was among the French Catholic intelligentsia, and how nefarious it was in the opinion of the Church.

Not much of this glamour has remained. Unlike, for instance, his contemporary Edmund Husserl, Bergson has survived only as a dead classic. Even in France interest in his work is only residual. To be sure, sometimes, somewhere, someone writes a doctoral thesis on 'Bergsonism', yet it may fairly be said that today's philosophers, both in their research and in their teaching, are almost entirely indifferent to his legacy. Some of Bergson's tenets and insights have survived in existential philosophy, but in a context which has utterly altered their meaning. Both the immense impact of his ideas and its subsequent disappearance are noteworthy as cultural phenomena and have to be seen as an aspect of general changes in the European mind within the last half-century.

In his essay *Philosophical Intuition* (1911), Bergson remarks that each great philosopher has only one thing to say, and more often than not gets no further than an attempt to express it. This central insight is always quite simple, yet the philosopher usually only circles around it, conceals it in various complicated constructions and finally fails to make it explicit, so that this task is left to his readers and commentators.

If we attempt to apply Bergson's remark to himself, we may sum up his philosophy in a single idea: time is real. Thus expressed, this statement does not sound particularly enlightening, original, or exciting. Once we explore its meaning, however, it turns out to be a kernel from which an entire new world picture might be developed.

To say that time is real is to say, first, that the future does not exist in any sense. This is by no means a trivial point, according to Bergson, since for a determinist every event merely unfolds the ready-made reality hidden in existing conditions; the course of events consists, as it were, in displaying a destiny written in advance for all eternity, as if time were only a machine to unwind a film reel which has been there all along, with its entire story. For Bergson, on the contrary, the life of the universe is a creative process, whereby something new and thus unpredictable appears at every moment.

This implies, secondly, that no physical equations – whether of classical or of relativist physics – deal with, or give us access to, time proper; the time of physics is not real. Both in science and in our daily life we perceive time as if it were another kind of space: a set of homogeneous segments placed next to each other and together composing an indefinitely long line. This time is an artificial, abstract concoction that we need for practical purposes; nothing would change in physical equations if the whole of reality were displayed simultaneously in one single picture. Real time, called by Bergson *durée* (which 'duration' does not render quite adequately), is neither homogeneous nor divisible; it is not a property abstracted from movement but it is in fact what each of us is: we know it intuitively, from direct experience.

Thirdly, real time is therefore possible only through memory, in which the past is accumulated in its fullness. In the abstract time of physics, nothing of one segment is preserved in the subsequent ones; they are juxtaposed in an indifferent succession. In the actual *durée* nothing is lost, but nothing is reversible either: each moment carries within it the entire flow of the past and each is new and unrepeatable. Since the matter of the past perishes, but the memory of it does not, and since memory is not an aspect of matter, it is likely that the human mind is largely independent of body and can survive its destruction.

Fourthly, if real time has the characteristics of memory, if its nature is psychological, it appears that, to the extent that we may speak of a time-bound universe, the evolution of the universe displays mind-like properties. Bergson aims to prove that this is indeed the case, and, further, that

3

evolutionary processes, in particular the evolution of organic matter, are actually the work of mind. The theory of evolution is to be incorporated into an essentially spiritualist picture of the world, according to which matter itself is intelligible only within the framework of a creative divine spirit.

So conceived, the seemingly simple idea that 'time is real' is certainly not an uncontroversial truism. Its persuasive power depended of course on the force of the arguments Bergson employed. He wanted to remain as close as possible to experience: in contrast to the mainstream of European philosophy, he believed that metaphysics both is possible and can be built on the basis of the existing stock of empirical science, if only we are able to discard philosophical prejudices which prevent us from seeing its results in their purity and which we unconsciously insert into the data of experience. When he criticized associationist psychology, the materialist theory of mind, the mechanist concept of evolution, and the purely sociological interpretation of religion – the four major topics of his four major works – he kept arguing that all the doctrines he attacked, far from deriving from an impartial inquiry into empirical material, imposed on this material old philosophical prejudices, thereby distorting its meaning. His calling, as he saw it, was not to spin new speculative constructions, but to remain faithful to what direct experience provides us with. He fought against positivists and Kantians, two major currents of the French, and indeed the European, philosophy of his formative years. Unlike the former, he wanted to prove that traditional metaphysical questions are legitimate and soluble. Unlike the latter, he argued that to solve them we need only to listen attentively to the voice of experience and that, if there is an a priori framework of mind, it is there for practical expediency, rather that for cognitive purposes.

This was the reason that his philosophy was hailed by so many people as an instrument of 'liberation' -- a word frequently used by the witnesses of those days, like Jacques Maritain (later one of Bergson's most severe critics) or Charles Péguy. But from what was Bergson supposed to have 'liberated' French intellectual life? From scientism and Taine's or Renan's 'religion of science', from the belief that natural science, as it was constituted in the second half of the nineteenth century, had provided us with an unsurpassed model of genuine knowledge, that all criteria of validity and truth had been established in the procedures of empirical and mathematical science and that all cognitive results worthy of this name derive their legitimacy from the correct application of these criteria. From mechanism, that is, from the belief that all events that occur in the universe consist of the spatial displacement of material particles according to the laws of Newtonian mechanics and that, consequently, it is the natural ideal of all sciences – in particular of the life sciences – to explain by those laws all the phenomena they study, and so ultimately to reduce all branches of knowledge to physics. From the determinists' contention that the future has always been settled in all its details, in particular that our use of terms such as 'free choice' or 'creativity' results from our ignorance of causes and that in principle any given state of the universe can be repeated, that no changes are absolutely irreversible. From the materialists' interpretation of mental phenomena, from the attempts to explain the life of the mind by the laws of association. From the positivist dismissal of all the questions dealing with the meaning of life, the calling of humanity, the divine origin of the universe, the qualitative distinctions between various forms of being. From the

Kantian doctrine that our knowledge consists in synthesizing the contingent stuff of perception with the help of the necessary forms that our intellect imposes on it, whereby a direct contact of mind with reality becomes impossible.

While he opposed to the prevailing tendency of the time his metaphysics of creativity, novelty, and of the qualitative growth of the universe, Bergson did not simply react to what he believed was wrong with the European mind. He wanted to absorb the entire body of science which had been built up in the preceding decades and free it from arbitrary philosophical ingredients. He never dismissed the value of science and of analytical reason; he argued instead that by their very nature they are incapable of grasping the facts of creativity and of time. He did not question the findings of the then existing physiology of the brain, the theory of evolution, or the sociological investigation of religious phenomena; he tried to show that the results of all these inquiries, when inspected by an unprejudiced mind, far from ruling out the purposeful order of the universe, the independence of soul from body, the presence of an expanding divine energy in the world, and our possible contact with the source of Being, do in fact strongly suggest, though not necessarily entail, a metaphysics for which all these tenets provide the foundation. His favourite method of analysis was what he called *recoupage*: when trying to answer a question he confronted two existing solutions embedded in opposite conceptual systems and then asked at what point they overlapped, that is, what they had in common, whereupon he showed that they shared a false assumption concealed in the very way they phrased the question. Thus he was ready to attack the root of the problem. He employed this procedure to demonstrate that both determinists and inderterminists admit the same wrong presupposition and so do both materialists and adherents of psycho-physical parallelism, both mechanists and the advocates of teleology, both realists and idealists.

The biological approach

A curious coincidence: in 1859, the same year that Darwin's *On the Origin of the Species* appeared (and, it might be added, Marx's *Critique of Political Economy* with its famous exposition of historical materialism), Henri Bergson and Edmund Husserl were born – two most important thinkers who, from entirely different perspectives, were to react to the changes that affected the European mind as a result of Darwin's work. (Freud, another great subversive, had been born three years earlier.)

Among the philosophical effects of the theory of evolution was a shift from the Cartesian and Kantian tradition to an approach whose core was the naturalization of consciousness: the human mind, including its cognitive behaviour, has to be seen as an organ of the body, as an instrument of self-defence helping our organism in the struggle for survival against the environment. The only meaning of our acts of perception consists in restoring the equilibrium that is unceasingly disturbed by external stimuli, and the only purpose of our conceptual apparatus is to store the acquired results of experience in the abbreviated form of abstract notions. Thus the 'validity' of our knowledge consists in its biological usefulness; the question about 'truth' in the traditional sense of an 'adaequatio', a congruence between the world in itself and its picture in the mind, is to be given up as a metaphysical superstition, along with the ideas of 'substance', 'cause', and 'ego' – all of which David Hume had rightly done away with – and indeed along with the very distinction between mental and physical facts or between the internal and the

7

external world. These arguments, upheld by empiriocritics – Avenarius and Mach above all – amounted not only to smashing the entire body of traditional metaphysics, but to making nonsense of all epistemological questions. The upshot was an unrestrictedly relativist, pragmatic concept of knowledge, identified with the usefulness of cognitive acts. Husserl reacted to the sceptical results of this biological approach by pointing out the unavoidable vicious circle of radical relativism. Its advocates urge that 'truth' is only an aspect of biologically functional behaviour, yet they base their arguments upon scientific findings which they accept as true in the normal sense; they seek an experience cleansed of abstract conceptual insertions, yet they have to employ those abstract devices in order to define what is or is not genuinely pure experience. Husserl also tried to construct the pure subject of cognition whose cognitive acts do not depend on the entire biological, social, psychological or historical framework which moulds the way we interpret our daily experience.

Bergson, by contrast, was ready to assimilate the biological approach into the analysis of knowledge; yet he imposed on it two important restrictions which fundamentally altered its sense. He argued first, that our analytical mind, both in everyday life and in scientific investigation, is essentially a practical organ of 'life': it is not interested in reality as it truly is but only in its potential utility; it cuts up and reconstructs the world not according to the world's natural fibres, as it were, but according to human biological needs. There is nevertheless another way we can commune with reality itself, by intuition, not by analysis. Secondly, 'life' itself is not a contingent by-product of physical laws and does not merely proceed in conformity with the Darwinian rules of the mechanical elimination of the maladjusted: it is a manifestation of creative energy. Though the human mind is a work of biological evolution, this evolution itself is the work of mind.

New trends in European thought

We used to perceive Bergson's philosophy, retrospectively, as the theoretical expression, no doubt the most salient, of a cultural trend which swept through Europe from the 1890s onwards and which is sometimes labelled 'modernism' or 'neo-Romanticism'. This attack had as its main targets mechanism and determinism in philosophy, utilitarianism in ethics, optimistic confidence in progress, naturalism and the didactic spirit in literature, collectivism in political ideologies. 'Life' was the most powerful catchword of the age, and 'life' was opposed not only to inert matter, but to the supremacy of calculating reason and to the monopoly of the analytical spirit. Religious and metaphysical mysteries, seemingly banished for ever by the irreversible verdict of physics and chemistry, surfaced again to reassert their inalienable rights: Reason itself, the claims of rationalists notwithstanding, turned out to be just an organ of life, and not the supreme judge which separated hard reality from figments of the imagination. The world, it was claimed, refuses to be confined to the artificial limits that the sciences had imposed on it; its mysterious and elusive facets keep haunting our experience, whatever the rationalists might decree. Art nouveau shaped objects in everyday use to make them similar to plants and efface the borderline between nature and the technological efforts of man. The tendency of the *Zeitgeist* was, on the one hand, to perceive the world as permeated by quasi-subjective energies, and, on the other, to stress the unity of this all-pervading spirit in which the human personality seemed to dissolve, carried away by the 'nostalgia of the ocean'. One could observe, along with the popularity of Schopenhauer and Nietzsche, an intense interest in oriental religions and legends, and in explorations of the occult. A remote echo of this 'restitution of subjectivity' may even be heard in the abandonment of the nineteenth-century determinist gospel and the emergence of new 'voluntarist' trends in socialist movements (whose exponents included Lenin, Mussolini, and Sorel).

Bergson's philosophy has repeatedly been associated with Maeterlinck's dramas, with their hinting at mysterious forces which tragically and irresistibly shape human destinies; with Debussy's music; with Symbolist poetry; with Proust's novels, in their depiction of the indestructible persistence of memory. Such associations are notoriously imprecise, as are all attempts to grasp and to describe the leading trends in the mentality of an age; they are not useless, though, and not necessarily arbitrary. That the striking popularity of a philosopher is never based on his own merit alone, seems even to be trivially true, however much analytically oriented thinkers might dislike the quest for the meaning of a philosophy in the cultural conditions of its emergence and influence ('philosophy is true or false, music is not').

Yet participation in the *Zeitgeist* is not a conscious intention, at least not in the case of original thinkers who challenge specific problems and who find themselves unexpectedly in the company of people working in entirely different areas. Bergson's own path began with his effort to grapple with Zeno's paradoxes, which he wanted to explain to his high-school pupils; a problem which certainly bothered few of those who eminently helped to build, with him, 'the spirit of the era'. William James, the only contemporary philosopher who, Bergson felt, moved in a similar direction – they exchanged letters and their respective books with a feeling of mutual sympathy – started with questions of an entirely different kind. People who, separately and often without being aware of the others' existence, design the shape of a recognizable entity in the history of culture meet, as it were, in an impersonal spiritual space which seems to have been waiting for a specific content, and the content comes from unconnected concerns and disparate sources.

It needs to be mentioned, however, that neither Bergson nor James shared the gloomy mood of so many of their contemporaries who anticipated the imminent unhappy end of the civilization in which they lived: the philosophy of both was fundamentally optimistic.

2 Time and immobility

The fallacy of spatial analogies

No one who peruses Bergson's works in chronological sequence can fail to notice the extraordinary consistency in his development. This does not mean that we perceive the whole as a building planned in advance; it was rather – as Gabriel Marcel put it – a development of the kind Bergson himself depicted in *Creative Evolution*: a process driven uninterruptedly by the same initial effort, but whose result cannot be known before it actually emerges. Nor does this mean that we should not look for ambiguities or perhaps even contradictions in his work; if there are contradictions, however, we should expect to explain them in terms of the same original drive (*élan*).

Bergson was very conscious of what constituted the core of his thinking, and on various occasions he corrected his critics or commentators by pointing it out. This is how he explained the 'leading idea of all [his] research' in a letter of 1923:

> whereas through all our natural abilities of perceiving and conceiving, which are constructed with the necessity of action in sight, we believe that immobility is as real as movement (we even believe that the former is fundamental and prior to the latter, and that movement is 'added' to it), we may find a solution to philosophical problems only if we succeed, by a reversal of these mental habits, to see in mobility the only reality that is given. Immobility is but a picture (in the

photographic sense of the word) taken of reality by our mind. (W 3.560)

A philosopher does not need to be infallible in perceiving the hierarchical order of his own thought, and nothing prevents us from reconstructing it differently, yet in Bergson's case there is little doubt about the soundness of his self-interpretation.

It is generally accepted that the four major books (*Essay on the Immediate Data of Consciousness, Matter and Memory, Creative Evolution,* and *Two Sources of Morals and Religion*) make up the whole of Bergson's philosophy. Numerous essays, articles, and lectures are important, to be sure, in that they throw light on some consequences of his ideas or provide a more precise explanation for them, yet they hardly alter the general picture. And it has often been noticed that in Bergson's work 'the whole' is omnipresent, so to speak, and informs every page, no matter what the ostensible subject.

In the early stages of his intellectual development, Bergson was a follower of Spencer, the great guiding spirit of post-Darwinian philosophy; he admired him for his constant effort to stay close to empirical material, and for his bold attempt to make evolution the guiding principle of philosophical thinking. But he was soon to come to the conclusion that Spencer had remained within the old mechanistic categories and was therefore incapable of grasping either the specificity of the life process or the distinction between the real time of consciousness and the abstract time of physics; thus the crucial phenomenon of novelty was beyond his reach.

As mentioned above, Bergson's early philosophical development was occasioned by his attempt to understand properly what was wrong with Zeno's paradoxes. Why does it appear plausible to argue that Achilles will never be able to catch up with the tortoise, given that we know for certain that he can? Bergson frequently returned to Eleatic thought in his books and articles and he saw in Zeno's paradoxes a paradigm of a certain way of thinking which our intelligence naturally follows because this suits its practical, action-oriented nature.

Let us recall the most famous paradox. If the tortoise is ahead of Achilles at a certain moment, Achilles will never be able to catch up with it: by the time he arrives at the point where the tortoise had previously stood, the animal will already have moved on, however slowly, and by the time Achilles reaches this next point, the tortoise will have moved again, and so on *ad infinitum*. The error of this reasoning, according to Bergson, is that Zeno identifies indivisible and *sui generis* acts of movement with the divisible and homogeneous space in which they occur. Geometrical space is indeed infinitely divisible, and we can conceive the trajectory of a moving body as a collection of segments, the number of which we can augment indefinitely, thereby making movement impossible (in the extreme version the body, if it is to move, has to run through an infinite series of points which make up any segment of the line). In reality each movement made by Achilles or the tortoise is a single, indivisible act, and what Zeno effectively proves is that we can never reconstruct the movement from a series of immobile states. The same confusion reigns in all of Zeno's arguments. Take, for instance, his paradox of the arrow. If Zeno's arrow really *were* at a certain point at every moment in its trajectory, it would indeed be immobile at every moment; consequently it would be immobile for ever. But the moving arrow never *is* at any certain point, and we can understand this easily if, instead of starting with space, we take the fact of movement as the original, irreducible reality.

In his *Essay*, Bergson aims to show that the confusion of movement and time with space is at the source of our inability to grasp both the real time we experience in our own conscious life, and the very nature of human freedom. He discusses first our confusion of the degrees of intensity of our psychological states in terms of increase or decrease in size as if, for instance, a greater sadness contained in it a lesser sadness, not unlike the way in which a higher number contains any lower one. Yet the intensity of emotions and sensations has nothing to do with numbers or size; no psychological experience is quantitatively comparable to another. Even the sensations associated with muscular effort cannot be described in quantitative terms: an increased effort of the muscles is perceived, rather, as an increase in the number of peripheral sensations and in the qualitative changes in some of them. There is no such thing as a 'greater' or 'smaller' anger, if we mean by this a difference in size; the difference is qualitative, and attempts to give it a numerical expression derive from the confusion of an emotion with its causes or with its physiological effects. The sensations of cold and heat do not differ from each other according to the degrees on a thermometer. All simple psychological facts are pure qualities.

The same confusion lies at the bottom of our abstract concept of time, and consists in reducing a single, indivisible quality to a number of units in a homogeneous entity such as space, or a series of numbers. Abstract, homogeneous, and infinitely divisible time is a sign, a symbolic representation of the real *durée*, and not the *durée* itself, which has no parts or segments external to each other; in our experience of time, no separation of this kind can be established between the present and previous states.

Still, the confusion is natural and very useful, indeed indispensable. We perceive pure *durée* when we concentrate on our internal experience only, leaving aside the world of things among which we live, abandoning the practical orientation of the mind, and taking instead an attitude of disinterested contemplation. But our intelligence is constructed in such a way as to be able to deal adequately with inert matter and to organize it according to the needs of life; it is primarily an organ of survival and of progress in technical skills. Its tendency is to reduce qualities to quantitative differences, new phenomena to old patterns, the unique to the repeatable and abstract, time to space. Real time being the form *par excellence* of our conscious life, we have to attribute a temporal dimension to things themselves in order to manipulate them, whereupon we project this measurable time back on to ourselves. In reality, there is no time in matter. When I follow the movement of a hand on a clock, I do not measure *durée*; without me, the observer, there would be no real transition from one position of the hand to another: 'the interval of the *durée* exists only for us, and because of the mutual penetration of our conscious states; outside us one would find nothing but space, and thus simultaneities, of which one may not even say that they objectively succeed each other, as any succession is conceived of by comparing the present to the past' (E 86).

In other words, it is fair to say that, according to Bergson, if time is real, the past does not exist except in memory. Indeed, what *was*, no longer *is*, by definition. If we could imagine a world without a conscious observer (which we cannot do, of course, as the act of our imagination inevitably adds the observer), this world would be perfectly identical with itself at every moment, but there would be no transition from one moment to another. Only the memory and thus consciousness maintains the continuity of the world.

Bergson was by no means the first to have tried to describe this mystery of time and its mind-related nature. St Augustine did it in a famous chapter of the *Confessions* and it is strange that Bergson, who often quoted Plato, Aristotle, Descartes, Spinoza, Leibniz, and Kant, never made reference to this splendid text which, at various points, is so close to his own struggling with the same intractable puzzle. The only conceivable reason is that Bergson had simply never heard of, let alone read, the *Confessions*.

Our inborn Platonism

Once we realize that movement and real – that is, experienced – time are not divisible, and not reducible to the space in which the movement occurs, that space and time are radically different entities whose nature we cannot grasp – as Leibniz and Kant would have it – in analogous conceptual categories, we see that the question of determinism must be posed in new terms and that in phrasing it we have to be aware of the unavoidable limits of language.

Each of us is a body among bodies, and our mind, in so far as it is an organ of life, acts according to the body's needs. That in us which obeys the laws of matter makes up the 'superficial self'; it conceives of itself as a part of the spatially homogeneous universe. The 'profound self', the core of personality, is not a tool of life, nor an aspect of our practical efforts, whether individual or social; more often than not we are not aware of it, and there is no pressing reason that we should be, absorbed as we are in our everyday concerns to survive. Both selves are layers of the same stream of consciousness, even though the 'superficial self' is to be seen as an impersonal part of the person. Therefore, all the expressions of consciousness, our sensations, emotions, and ideas, 'display a double aspect: one is clear, precise, and impersonal; the other is confused, infinitely mobile, and inexpressible, because language cannot grasp it without immobilizing its mobility' (E 96).

This inability of language to describe the 'profound self', far from being a contingent defect, reveals the very nature of our linguistic apparatus: language, as a part of our intelligence, is essentially a set of abstract signs; its task is to classify objects, to dissolve them into conceptual classes; uniqueness, unless it is an empirically unique collection of abstracts, is beyond its reach. No real object can be exhaustively depicted by the enumeration of the various classes to which it belongs, as their number is infinite. And there is no reason why we should try to do this: both our perception and our language seek to pick out those aspects of the world which are relevant to our practical needs and to leave aside everything else. In *Creative Evolution* Bergson compares our mind to a cinematographic mechanism: it decomposes movement into a finite number of immobile pictures on a film, and reconstructs it afterwards.

All this can be expressed by saying that we are born Platonists: our mind spontaneously assumes that abstract entities are more real than, and prior to, individual objects and that there is less to movement than to mobility, that the former is a degradation of the latter. This Platonism is an innate characteristic of our intellect and derives from the utilitarian nature of thought. In order to live and to improve our skills we have to dissect the world into fragments which bear no resemblance to real things, as real things are not sets of general notions. Our linguistic network is bound to immobilize the experience of time, and it makes the expression of change, of mobility as such, simply impracticable.

We shall see that this dichotomy is less rigid than it appears: our intelligence can make an effort to go beyond itself, and our language – built as it is on spatial relationships – can overcome to some extent its limitations and open a path to another, non-Platonic understanding of reality. This is in fact how Bergson himself tried to employ language; and this is what poets do.

Our freedom

It is in terms of the 'profound self' which is ultimately identical with pure *durée* that the quest for freedom can start.

Mechanistic determinism implies that all our conscious states are literal and perfect translations of the spatial movements that occur in our body or in the nervous system. This, however, is an arbitrary philosophical prejudice which not only is not, but can never be, borne out by experience. The point is not only that all the correspondences – obvious and less obvious – between our conscious acts and their physical 'background' can never cancel the irreducibility of the simplest conscious event and convince us that what we are conscious of are molecular motions in our brain. Bergson insists rather on a discussion between determinists and their adversaries in the psychological terms of motivations and decisions. For determinists the 'psychological factors' in our decisions are conflicting forces of various strengths, the 'free' decision being nothing more than the victory of the strongest over the weaker. Thus they believe that in a given psychological situation which consists of the tension of opposite forces, only one outcome is possible. The indeterminists, on the other hand, try to show that many results are equally possible and that the final upshot (a decision following our deliberations and hesitations) is unpredictable. For both, our conscious acts are preceded by mechanical oscillations; both place themselves at a point when the act has already been performed and try to reconstruct its antecedents. Both, in other words, fail to perceive the reality of time, and replace it by spatial representations, whereas in fact our deliberations make up an indivisible dynamic process. In predicting the future behaviour of an individual we actually do nothing more than express our opinion of his present character and dispositions. We could really predict the behaviour of another person only if we identified ourselves entirely with him, including his past, but then the 'prediction' would be the very performance of the 'predicted' act, whereas the supposed prediction from outside consists in an attempt to reduce real *durée* to what it radically is not: a collection of measurable forces. The very concepts of prediction and causality, taken from the realm of physics, are meaningless when applied to consciousness.

The fundamental impossibility of psychological determinism is rooted in the continuity of psychological life. A determinist states that, in the same conditions, the same phenomena occur. However, the same conditions can never, by definition, obtain in the life of the self, because each, artificially isolated, moment of its duration includes the entire past, which is, consequently, different for each moment. By contrast with the universe of abstract equations, the same situation never occurs twice in the being endowed with memory; since real time is absolutely irreversible, neither the same cause nor the same effect can ever reappear in experience.

It seems that Bergson's theory of freedom may be restated

as follows: if we examine the questions of freedom and necessity on the implicit or explicit assumption that physical and mental events are fundamentally of the same nature, and that the categories of cause and effect may be applied to them in the same sense, the general doctrine of determinism cannot be proved, to be sure, but neither can it be refuted. A determinist can always argue that the supposedly free aspects of some events or acts are just so many lacunae in our knowledge, and this hypothesis, though unprovable, could pass for a natural guiding rule of scientific inquiry. Indeterminists who look for a mysterious margin of causal emptiness within a world governed by necessity are in a hopeless position precisely because they share with their adversaries the belief that all the events under scrutiny, whether in the realm of matter or in that of consciousness, succeed each other in the same homogeneous temporal milieu and that cause–effect relationships have the same meaning in both areas.

All the components of the question of freedom are altered once we realize that real temporal succession occurs only in the mind and is projected on to matter. In real time, in the life of consciousness, there is a perfect continuity, and our self is at every moment, as it were, in a state of being born, absorbing its past and creating its future; it has a history, no doubt, it even *is* its history stored in memory, but it cannot go through the same state again; such a miracle would amount to the reversal of time.

To define freedom as a hole in the compact mass of things is to deny it from the outset. We are free by being conscious, by producing time, and not by escaping from physical causality, where only simultaneity appears, not the present as opposed to the past. 'In consciousness we find states which succeed each other without being distinct from each other; and in space, simultaneities which are distinct from,

21

without succeeding, each other' (E 171).

This should not suggest that we are equally free at every moment of our lives. Since a surface-layer of consciousness is immersed in our physical coexistence with things, it is understandable that freedom allows of degrees. We are free whenever we wish, says Bergson, but we do so only rarely. 'We are free when our acts emanate from the whole of our personality, when they express it and when they have this kind of indefinable resemblance to it that we see sometimes between a work and the artist' (E 129).

It is inaccurate to talk about the 'problem of freedom' because even in events which involve the full intensity of freedom the latter cannot be observed and established as a fact 'from outside'. Having no means of living another person's conscious life, I cannot grasp his freedom as an empirical fact and thus, when inspecting another personality, I naturally convert it into a thing, which it is as little as myself, and impose on it the conceptual method I employ when dealing with objects: homogeneous time, separable events, relations of cause and effect.

It is therefore fair to say that in Bergson's analysis freedom is both unquestionably certain and utterly unprovable in the sense which the word 'to prove' has acquired in scientific inquiry.

This might suggest that time is imprisoned within 'my' conscious *durée* and the question naturally arises: how is a common time for the human community possible at all? We shall deal with this riddle later on.

The founding tenets of Bergson's philosophy have thus been laid down in his first work: the distinction between real and abstract time is tantamount to the opposition between what is specifically human and what is physical, between consciousness and inert matter; it reveals the practical nature of intelligence. The distinction is a matter of simple experience: once we realize that the flow of time is the life-form *par excellence* of consciousness and that the past–present–future structure is its exclusive characteristic, we see at once that the events of consciousness are absolutely irreducible to physical ones and that any description of the former in terms of the latter is impossible and absurd. That we nevertheless attempt such a description, and that philosophy teems with such attempts, is to be explained by the fact that our intellect naturally thinks of the world in terms of practical manipulation and that I have no access to a consciousness other than my own. In spite of the limits of our language, modelled as it is on spatial relationships, we are able to unmask the natural error of both philosophy and of everyday thinking and, instead of reducing movement to an infinite series of immobile states, and the acts of the self to physical events, to grasp mobility and conscious experience as primary data and to describe everything else in relation to them.

The sharp dichotomy set out by Bergson between what is human, or timebound, and what is mechanical, is mitigated in the course of further analysis when it turns out that the self has an aspect which participates in the realm of matter. We shall see later on that the dichotomy is blurred, too, in the other direction: in matter we perceive a kind of participation in spirit. All of Bergson's other distinctions meet with the same fate: at the outset they seem clear-cut and deprived of all intermediate zones, yet in the final analysis we see that each side carries within it a shadow of the other. This is the case, among others, of the intuition–analysis dichotomy.

3   Intuition and intellect

Two kinds of our acquaintance with the world

Bergson has been systematically labelled an 'irrationalist', and the most frequently quoted evidence for this accusation comes from his essay *Introduction to Metaphysics* (1903). Though apparently consistent with other writings, many of which repeat the same tenets, this essay used to be singled out by rationalist critics because of some especially strong formulas and because 'intuition' was used in it as a leading battle-cry.

We get to know a thing, Bergson says, either by circling around it or by entering into it. If we stay outside, the result depends on our standpoint and is expressed in symbols, whereas in the second kind of cognition we follow the life of the thing in an empathic identification with it. In the first approach – analysis – I am unable to grasp, let alone express, the uniqueness of the object; I have to decompose it into elements which I describe only in terms already known to me. Thus I do not deal with reality itself, I merely isolate its repeatable aspects, each of them relative to my angle of perception. The second approach alone enables me to reach the reality which does not depend on my position and is, in that sense, absolute. This approach – intuition – is 'a sympathy whereby one carries oneself into the interior of an object to coincide with what is unique and therefore inexpressible in it. Analysis, on the other hand, is an operation which reduces the object to elements that are known and that the object has in common with others' (P 181). When we move our hand, we perceive our performance 'from inside' as one simple act, whereas its description 'from without' would necessarily be incomplete.

The reality I am certainly capable of grasping by intuition is myself. I coincide with my own time and I realize that each state of my consciousness is unique, as it absorbs the past which by definition is constantly growing; indeed we can distinguish separate segments of *durée* only after they have gone into the past. Thus consciousness cannot be identical during two consecutive moments; its continuity is in memory or, as Bergson puts it, 'consciousness means memory' (P 183).

Analysis is essentially selection. Our mind concentrates on those aspects of things that are practically important, and discards the others; in reality, however, there is no distinction between an object and its properties. To be sure, the analytical approach is a condition of our survival: we could not live and act if we did not have at our disposal a mechanism whereby things are cut up, so to speak, into many aspects, according to a hierarchy of their practical relevance to our lives. The principles of those cutting operations are embedded in our conceptual instrumentarium: the value of abstract concepts derives from the fact that they decompose the world into elements relative to human needs; in cognitive terms they provide us with shadows instead of a body, and even our ordinary sense-perception is likewise selective. 'Selective' means distorting. The unrepeatable, the unique, and thus the real, is beyond the reach of analysis and of symbolic representation. Intuition does what intelligence never can: it brings us into the world as it is, irrespective of utilitarian considerations.

The sciences are natural products of the analytical mind, and suffer all its limitations. They are designed at the outset for manipulation; their purpose is to isolate what is common in things and what can therefore be immobilized in laws, measured, made timeless, included in our desire to predict events and to influence them to suit our wishes. Empirical or speculative psychology does not differ in this respect from other branches of science. Its aim is to dissolve the unique and indivisible whole of personality into conceptual units, whereupon it treats them as if they were real parts of a person, rather than artificially fabricated tools of analysis. And yet the most insignificant and trivial act of consciousness is an expression of personality; it includes its entire past and present and, consequently, can be understood only by reference to this relationship. Both empiricists and rationalists fall prey to the same error: they conceive of these symbolic fabrications as real pieces of consciousness and try to use the former to reconstruct the latter, thus losing the 'concrete unity' of human existence. The 'self' or 'ego' is to them merely a convenient word, having little to do with a person's genuine *durée*. The same illusion haunts all our scientific endeavours: we either attempt to reduce movement to a series of immobile states (as empiricists do) or, in a rationalist manner, to define the self as an absence of characteristics, an empty verbal unit, a form without substance. 'But what true empiricism aims at is to follow as closely as possible the original itself, to deepen its life and, by a kind of ''spiritual auscultation'', to feel its soul pulsate, and this true empiricism is true metaphysics' (P 196). When dealing with a new object, this empiricism must make an absolutely new effort, start everything afresh; it cannot operate with ready-made general concepts.

We must not suppose that analytical knowledge, restricted by utilitarian concerns and therefore supplying us with pragmatic views of reality, rather than with knowledge proper, is at least clear and precise, whereas intuition remains obscure and vague. Such an assessment involves the previous acceptance of analytical prejudices. We cannot claim that movement is more obscure or more difficult to grasp than immobility unless we believe that the latter is logically or empirically prior, which is what our intelligence is prone to believe. Once we place ourselves in the position of a disinterested observer and dismiss the natural habits of mind, we see easily that movement and time are *the* reality we deal with directly, in the simplicity of unmediated contact.

There is nothing logically compelling in the claim that there are selves – *durées* – other than mine, but we know from experience that there are many, both on a lower and on a higher level than our own. My experience of time is not self-contained, and intuition reaches other beings in an unshakeable certainty. We can go beyond ourselves and extend our time in both directions: the way down leads towards pure homogeneity or pure repetitiveness, that is, materiality; on the way up we come closer and closer to living eternity. The movement of our intuition between these two extremes is metaphysics.

'Irrationalist'

In what sense does Bergson's doctrine deserve the label 'irrationalism' and if the name is suitable, in what sense does it amount to an accusation?

The word 'irrationalism' is occasionally applied to the claim that the most vital questions concerning the world and the human position in it are insoluble, that no unifying order can be discovered in the universe, that our reason is constantly assailed by mysteries which it is never able to fathom or, in an extreme version, that truth in the sense of congruence is just a wishful illusion. In this sense the label clearly does not fit Bergson's thought. His main purpose is

27

to show, on the contrary, that through intuitive empathy, 'absolute' reality can be revealed to us in its pristine purity, so to speak, unadulterated by practical considerations or by any a priori forms of intellect.

It seems that the main intention of those who make this charge against Bergson is to say: an irrationalist makes the claim that there are special forms of immediate cognition whose content is incommunicable, and that these forms are superior to those we can express in words and use for normal communication both in science and in everyday life. The knowledge the mystics claim to have acquired in direct communion with God is the paradigmatic example.

Even though Bergson in his later works discussed mystical experience and believed it to be genuine (in the sense in which mystics themselves described and interpreted it), he never pretended to have had this kind of experience; nor did he suggest that it might be universally accessible. The intuitive insight which he contrasted with analytical thinking seems to embrace various phenomena, of which mystical union is a rare and privileged instance.

Intuition is supposed to give us direct, yet not sensual, contact with reality, 'direct' meaning that it dispenses with abstract concepts. What is real is always unique. Bergson follows the nominalist tradition: abstractions have no equivalents in reality; since they serve to isolate, for practical purposes, certain qualities, and to group objects into classes, they are not, strictly speaking, cognitive instruments and do not open any avenues leading to genuine acquaintance with reality. On the assumption that our language is a collection of abstract symbols it appears that 'spiritual auscultation' is indeed inexpressible.

On this point it would be hard to clear Bergson of the charge of inconsistency. On the one hand he does assert that the insight he praises is indeed performed without symbols and that whatever cognitive gains we get from it are inevitably distorted in symbolic representation; in other words, intuition *is* incommunicable. On the other hand, he calls intuition a 'method', thereby suggesting that it might become a common good; he calls it 'metaphysics' as well, and it is hard to tell how an incommunicable metaphysics is conceivable. When Bergson examines, say, neurophysiological data in *Matter and Memory*, or biological findings in *Creative Evolution*, he opposes his own philosophical interpretation to other existing ones, yet he does not even pretend to report his personal experience of an incommunicable convergence with the objects under scrutiny. Right or wrong, his arguments remain within the normal, logical framework of discourse.

Certainly, to a rationalist, any claim to 'inexpressible knowledge' is an abomination, indeed the word itself is self-contradictory, as 'knowledge' refers properly to what can be uttered in correctly constructed sentences. It seems, however, that on the assumption that 'knowledge' is by definition propositional, rationalism is true because tautological, and it is far from obvious why 'irrationalism' thus negatively defined should necessarily be contemptible. The definitions implying that cognitive value derives solely from the correct application of the codes of modern empirical and mathematical science themselves require justification. Bergson was aware, of course, of this restrictive rule and he challenged it at its very root by pointing out that there are acts in which we gain access to reality and which nevertheless do not follow the procedures science has legitimized; why then must we declare them a priori cognitively void? The only reason is that they do not fit the purposes for which science has evolved: they cannot be employed in the effort of the human race to increase its power over matter. To conclude from this that they do not increase knowledge presupposes an arbitrary definition of 'knowledge' which we are free to dismiss.

Certainly, 'irrationalism' so conceived has often been attacked because of its harmful effects on the human mind: it teaches us, it has been alleged, scorn for science and logical rigour; it allows us to do away with intellectual discipline and to rely instead on unverifiable intuition, which by definition is infallible and cannot be a matter of argument.

If 'irrationalism' amounted to this sort of advice, it would indeed be easy to combat. Yet this is precisely the charge which cannot be made against Bergson. He never suggested that we replace scientific inquiry by a quasi-mystical contemplation and that instead of reasoning and experimenting we can solve a problem in mathematics or in physiology by intuiting the essence of the object. Towards science he showed humility and respect. Still, he tried to separate scientific inquiry from the metaphysical presuppositions hidden in the way in which it was interpreted, and he argued that traditional metaphysical questions, perfectly valid in themselves, are not soluble with the tools at the disposal of analytical reason.

> What is intelligence? The human way of thinking. It has been given to us as instinct to a bee, to direct our conduct. Since nature designed us to use and to master matter, intelligence develops easily only in space and feels itself at ease only in the unorganized world. It directs itself from the outset towards manufacturing, it reveals itself in an activity that anticipated the mechanical arts and in a language that announced science, whereas the rest in a primitive mentality is faith and tradition . . . Precise or vague, it is the attention

mind pays to matter. How then could mind still be intelligence once it turns towards itself? (P 84–5)

Intuition therefore is

the attention mind pays to itself in addition to its being focused on matter, its object. This additional attention can be methodically cultivated and developed. And so a science of mind, a true metaphysics, will evolve; it will define mind in a positive manner, instead of just denying it the characteristics, known to us, of matter. While we conceive of metaphysics in such a manner and assign to intuition the knowledge of mind, we take away nothing from intelligence, our claim being that metaphysics, which was the work of pure intelligence, eliminated time and therefore either denied mind or defined it by negation . . . On no point do we diminish intelligence; we do not expel it from any area it has occupied until now . . . Along with it, however, we find the existence of another faculty which is capable of another way of gaining knowledge. And so, we have on the one side science and mechanical art, which derive from pure intelligence, and, on the other, the metaphysics which appeals to intuition. Between these two extremes the science of moral, social, and even organic life will be located, the latter more intellectual, the former more intuitive. (P 85-6)

Bergson believed that the intuitive approach was not only different from, but 'superior' to, the analytical one, not in its efficacy, no doubt, but in that it consisted of an unmediated apprehension of the object. The ambiguities of his philosophy resulted from his somewhat careless general description which did not make quite clear how far intuition might be extended. Apart from introspective experience of time, Bergson's few examples refer to aesthetic perception or artistic creativity, both of them involving the operations of intuitions (a word which he was not happy about, but accepted for lack of a better expression). If a reader can, for example, identify with a character depicted in a novel and perceive the person from inside, all his acts and words, instead of being 'added' to the description, would naturally follow from this 'internal' understanding. A poet uses language in a way which in fact runs counter to its normal function in order to convey something that might evoke in the reader his own intuitive perception; the latter is not properly communicable but a great artist's effort can bring it closer to its expression than an analytical description might ever be able to.

The intuition/analysis dichotomy, like others of Bergson's oppositions, is thus less sharp than it might appear from his general definition. Intuition is a way of dealing with the life of the mind and its products. Occasionally, however, we are told, that we need intuition to grasp movement, the phenomena of life, and anything to the extent that it is unique; and that intuition is a kind of quasi-identification with the object. Yet, clearly, I cannot identify myself with a flying stone and an entomologist cannot become a mosquito in order to apprehend the nature of the creature. Moreover, if he could perform this transmutation, he would immediately cease to be an entomologist. Or, to take a less fantastic example, it is true that by eating an apple I get the kind of knowledge – taste – which I could never gain by analysing the apple chemically. This does not mean that I can replace the latter kind of knowledge with the former or that the former is somehow superior; here we simply have different acts resulting in different kinds of acquaintance with the object.

Bergson's position is as awkward as that of any philosopher trying to speak of what is admittedly inexpressible. St Augustine (in *De doctrina Christiana*) noted the contradiction involved in saying that 'God is ineffable': in uttering this sentence we say something about God, thus implying that he is not quite ineffable, after all. This is perhaps a paradox of self-reference which we might do away with by means of familiar distinctions between various levels of language. Not all philosophers, however, are likely to be satisfied with this solution; some will recognize that God is something that cannot be and, at the same time, has to be spoken of, that no logical devices will make this tension vanish and that a certain resulting intellectual discomfort cannot be removed from our thinking. This tension does not arise from our contingent logical ineptitude but from the intrinsic limitations of language as it tries to reach the absolute being. Nicholas of Cusa made perhaps the most intense effort to grapple with this intractable and inescapable trap to which a finite mind falls prey once it ventures into the realm of infinity. And even though Bergson's intuition does not necessarily intend to grasp the divine being – at least not ostensibly – the difficulty is of the same kind. The adjective 'concrete' is abstract, the adjective 'incommunicable' is communicable, the adjective 'unique' is general, and to utter the word 'intuition' is not itself an act of intuition. We cannot get rid of the barriers of language when we try to convey to others something that language is intrinsically not designed to deal with; we can use it none the less to produce various hints, metaphors, or aesthetically powerful images, in order to awaken in other people the faculty of intuition which, even if dormant, is a part of a universally human endowment.

Bergson

Comment

What Bergson had in mind when talking about intuition can be better understood in the context of his cosmology and his theory of life. Indeed, he himself was guilty of some misapprehension of his idea in that everything he had said on the subject before the publication of *Creative Evolution* had appeared outside this context. In the latter work, intuition is an aspect of the universal *élan vital*, or life-drive, which permeates the universe and guides the evolutionary process. In order to manufacture the highest forms of mind, nature had to use the material available, that is, inert matter; and in order to survive and evolve, living creatures had to have their mental equipment adjusted to a hostile environment. Nature's main effort was therefore to assure the highest degree of perfection in all the faculties which enable the human species efficiently to cope with, and to master, matter; language, science, technical skills, analytical reason, are components or products of this equipment, which is built according to the requirements matter imposes; and it is to these requirements that intuition has been almost – yet not entirely – sacrificed. To keep it alive, however, is of the utmost importance to humanity; throughout history it has been active in the most splendid achievements of man. And in employing it we are not seeking at all to replace our scientific effort. Intuition is one of the ways in which we commune with the *élan vital*, with the eternally creative source of being which is ultimately God himself. It is by intuition that we are able to discern the divine impulse in evolution and it is through this very understanding that we realize the function of intuition in the life of the cosmos. There is a circular argument here, Bergson admits, but an unavoidable one: we use our cognitive powers to gain insight into the life of the cosmos, and only this insight makes the function of our cognitive powers and their claims to validity intelligible. We might thus state – even though Bergson does not say so in so many words – that a *petitio principii*, or a Cartesian circle, is involved in any epistemology: the value of knowledge cannot be legitimized without inquiring into its origin and function, and such an inquiry cannot be made without first admitting that the cognitive instruments at our disposal are valid.

Bergson seems to believe that genuine acts of intuition break the circle; once they occur they need no further justification and leave no room for doubt. In them we see things 'from inside', we coincide with their time and thereby enter into the great creative stream of life which is conceived and propelled by a divine force. I can as little doubt the authenticity of intuitive insight as I can doubt whether I am alive or dead. And, despite the difficulties in conveying such acts to other people, there is no reason to refuse them cognitive value, except for the arbitrary restrictions of scientism.

Bergson's intuition is clearly far from the Cartesian notion of the same name. For Descartes, intuition was an act whereby we grasp the self-evidence radiating from the object itself; we get this kind of insight in assimilating, for instance, mathematical knowledge. For Bergson, it was an act of identification with the time in which the 'object' is immersed. Since time is psychological, everything seen in terms of time is mind or spirit. Is such an identification feasible at all, apart from the case of self-inspection? Mystical union with God, assuming that it is genuine, cannot be a matter for discussion among those who have not experienced it, let alone a 'method' to be recommended. That we might spiritually coincide with the movement of a bullet or a merry-go-round does not seem credible. There is no reason, however, to deny that we experience various forms of empathic understanding of other people's minds or of works of art, and that all attempts to convey the quality of such experience in verbal form are fatally clumsy and inadequate; apart from rationalist or behaviourist dogma, nothing compels us to deny that there is non-verbal communication with other persons, that it results in a feeling of mutual understanding and that in this kind of encounter we acquire knowledge which we did not have before. In the realm of direct or indirect human relationships these acts of empathy, which are not reducible to, or replaceable by, analytical effort, not only occur, but indeed make up the kernel of our personal and communal life within a culture. But words such as 'identification' or 'coincidence' are clearly too strong; cognitive acts imply a distinction between the perceiver and the object; any convergence can be only partial; only God, according to theologians, can and does know everything 'from inside'; and if an identification with the universal stream of life is possible, it would hardly differ – on Bergson's own assumption – from a mystical union.

Is the empathic insight 'better' than the analytical one? A futile question. One must first ask, better for what?

4   Mind and body

Two kinds of memory

At the beginning of his intellectual journey, Bergson, as he states, had no religious interests in the traditional sense. Later on, however, he was to admit that those traditional religious questions are the only *raison d'être* of philosophical reflection. In the essay 'Soul and Body' (1912) he wrote:

> Where do we come from? What are we doing here? Whither are we going? If philosophy had really nothing to say on these questions of vital interest, if it were not capable of clarifying them step by step as one clarifies biological or historical problems, if it could not benefit from more and more advancing experience, if it had to limit itself to bringing into oppositon those who assert and those who deny immortality for reasons that are inferred from the hypothetical essence of soul or body, it would be almost proper to say, reversing the meaning of Pascal's words, that the whole of philosophy is not worth one hour of trouble. (S 58)

Bergson did not ask such questions, at any rate not explicitly, when he was writing *Matter and Memory*; he was anxious not to go far beyond what could be gathered from the data accumulated by neurophysiologists. But in a number of subsequent essays he made a bolder attempt directly to confront the question of the soul's survival after death.

In *Matter and Memory*, the most learned and the most

difficult of his works, Bergson wants to show that mind – and by this he means memory – can by no means be considered a product of the brain; the latter is an organ of selection and not for manufacturing subjective mental acts; and he distinguishes between cerebral memory, which consists of the acquisition of habits, and pure recollection, which neither subsists in nor is created by the nervous system.

Bergson asserts the reality of both mind and matter, but his way of setting up the distinction between them aims to do away with all the established philosophical doctrines: idealism, realism, psychophysical parallelism. Whether we believe that states of consciousness are functions of the brain or that both kinds of events are translations of the same original into two different languages, we are presupposing that one can in principle come to know all the details of conscious life by examining the brain. However, Bergson says,

> it is indisputable that there is solidarity between a state of consciousness and the brain. There is also solidarity between clothes and the hook on which they hang; once we take away the hook, the clothes fall. Can we say that for this reason the form of the hook shapes the form of the clothes or gives us its anticipation? From the fact that a psychological event is attached to a state of the brain we cannot infer a 'parallelism' of the two series – the psychological and physiological. (M 4–5)

The main objects of Bergson's attention were the diseases and distortions of memory, especially those resulting from injuries of the brain. Not surprisingly, the inquiry into this kind of correlation supplied the advocates of the materialist interpretation of mind with their main argument: if some functions of the mind, particularly memory, are distorted or destroyed by lesions of the brain, then clearly they are nothing but its products or elements. This, according to Bergson, is a philosophical prejudice that is not only unsupported but contradicted by the experimental evidence.

He starts with the problem of perception. The images which make up the universe include a special component, my own body. My brain is a part of the material world; therefore it is absurd to suppose, with the idealists, that it produces, or is a condition of, all other images: if we cancel the world we cancel the brain with it. My body is a centre of action and cannot produce mental representations, whereas other bodies reflect my possible action on them. My perceptions are 'external' images in so far as they are relevant to my possible action.

Any image, however, is a part of two systems, each of them self-sufficient and independent from the other; one of them is science, and in this system the image has an absolute value (that is, it supposedly subsists in itself), whereas in the second system it is related to the central image, my body. An idealist derives the former from the latter, a materialist vice versa. Both believe that to perceive is to get to know and in this, according to Bergson, they are wrong. It is precisely when we climb up the ladder of evolution, follow the progressive specialization of tissues and the gradual emergence of the central nervous system, that we notice the eminently practical function of the brain: it acts like a telephone exchange, receiving messages from the peripheral sensors, selecting and dispatching them to the motor mechanisms; it is an organ of the body and its purpose is to co-ordinate external stimuli with responses. Perception itself does not consist of cognitive acts, it is too action-orientated. Pure perception would be what is purely 'external'; it is not really a part of the individual consciousness (between 'to be' and 'to be perceived' there is only a difference in degree, not in kind); but pure perception – which would be pure present – is an ideal entity; in fact each act of perception contains various layers of memory and it is memory which makes up its 'subjective side' and thus makes it conscious. Our actual representation of matter is a selection performed by the brain according to the needs of the body; what is practically uninteresting is eliminated both from memory and from the stuff of representation. The role of consciousness in acts of perception is 'to bind, by the continous string of memory, an uninterrupted series of instantaneous visions which are parts of things, rather than of ourselves' (M 67). That aspect of perception which comes from memory is added, as it were, to what matter provides, which suggests that memory is a kind of faculty independent from matter.

Why then does the stock of memory seem to follow changes in the brain? Why is it distorted or weakened as a result of brain injuries?

At this point we must distinguish more carefully between two kinds of memory. Suppose I try to learn a poem by heart and for this purpose I read it a number of times until I am capable of reciting it. Each of my readings is a single, unrepeatable act which my pure memory stores in all its details, whereas my ability to recite the poem is simply a habit, like other motor dispositions, one of many skills I acquire and deposit in my nervous system. These two kinds of memory are entirely different from each other. Pure recollection is an aspect of my consciousness, cerebral memory is an action-orientated modification of the body, the ability to repeat. The former, memory *par excellence*, preserves all the details of past experience, but not all of them are readily available at any moment: the brain is there, acting as a censor, so to speak, manipulating the resources of the past according to the practical needs of the body and using those recollections which may be useful in shedding light on the present situation and helping us to react to it.

The distinction between two kinds of memory, cerebral and spiritual, was drawn by Descartes, who attributed sense perception to the former and intellectual cognition to the latter; one should therefore expect a Cartesian disembodied mind to live in a world of pure concepts, not even remembering previous sensations. Bergson draws the distinction differently: everything perceived is preserved.

Brain injuries and other organic causes may, of course, directly damage the storage of motor memory and upset the control devices which select memory; various distortions of memory can result, but pure memory, the constantly growing mass of recollections – in other words, consciousness itself – is not destroyed. The mechanisms of remembering are affected by lesions of the cortex, but the repository of past experience is not. In real memory nothing is ever lost. Contrary to the view of many psychologists, it is utterly incredible, Bergson argues, to think that recollections are recorded physically in the brain, preserved there like sounds in the grooves of a gramophone record, and vanishing when the corresponding part of the tissue is destroyed. In some forms of verbal amnesia the gradual disappearance of memory follows a semantic order: first proper names are forgotten, then common nouns, then verbs. Can we imagine that words recorded in the brain substance are arranged and located according to grammatical patterns? In other forms of amnesia some letters of the alphabet are forgotten and not others: is it conceivable that the brain has separate cells to conserve each letter of the alphabet? And how does it happen that some areas affected by amnesia suddenly return to life? On the assumption that recollections are physically registered in the brain, we could not even explain how we are able to retain in the mind, say, the unified image of a person we know: each act of perceiving this person is by definition unique and unrepeatable, and our memory would have to store an indefinite number of such single acts, never a unitary picture.

Arguments of this kind support the conclusion that consciousness goes beyond the body. Indeed, if states of consciousness were nothing but replicas of what occurs in the nervous tissues, their very origin would be incomprehensible in terms of natural evolution. The organism could use all the devices at its disposal to react to the stimuli of the environment and to fight for survival; there would be no reason for these acts to be made conscious and duplicated in the form of 'mental events'. Both neurophysiological research and our experience of the inner self are understandable only on the assumption that matter and mind meet, as it were, in the nervous system; that the former, far from producing or storing the latter, limits it in line with biological defence mechanisms, and that the latter infinitely transcends the former. There is no doubt that consciousness is active in the behaviour of the body: it does not simply produce useless mental copies of physical events, and the mind is not just a passive observer of the body, as Spinoza would have it. The specific activity of the mind is to be understood in terms of its time structure and its freedom: 'The mind borrows from matter perceptions from which it takes its food and it gives them back to matter in the form of movements on which it imprints its freedom' (M 280).

This needs restating: it is through memory that time is real. Traces of the past recorded in matter are thought of as 'traces' only because consciousness is there to monitor changes; in itself, matter has no past or future. Hypothetical pure perception, limited to an abstractly concocted, dimensionless point in time, is an aspect of the material universe. In reality, there are no points, no separable events, and no atom-like components in the life of consciousness. Conciousness is an indivisible continuity of heterogeneous and unrepeatable qualities. Remembered images and anticipated actions are elements of all conscious acts, including perception. Sensations have spatial characteristics and are localized in the body; they provoke movements by the intermediary of the brain. Pure recollection is not part of the body; it is included in the body's actions in the form of images as a result of the selection operated by the brain; by becoming an image, the past is no longer pure recollection, but blends with the present.

These distinctions, according to Bergson, are perfectly in keeping with everything we know about psychological life. If children have an extraordinary capacity for memorizing things spontaneously, this is because their memory is not yet strictly co-ordinated with their bodily functions and is able to absorb and to keep active a lot of surplus stock; increasing co-ordination of recollections with movements is therefore associated with the apparent weakening of memory. When we are asleep, the control of memory by the brain is loosened and many past images float up to the surface of the mind, unchecked by the pressures of the organism. Within the same conceptual framework Bergson explained some parapsychological phenomena, such as telepathy, apparitions or phantoms of living people, and the feeling of *déjà vu*.

It is the essentially practical orientation of the brain which is responsible for the way the world, in our perception, is divided into separate objects which we subsequently order into abstract classes. In reality matter is not a collection of individual, well-shaped things; the universal interdependence of all its components makes the world one single thing. We nevertheless have to cut it into separate elements for practical reasons, since in our interaction with matter we obviously cannot take into account this infinite network of mutual influences. What seems to us an isolated object is not so much the work of nature as the result of the practical attention we direct at it. Thus we notice again the natural Platonic disposition of our mind: we divide up the world according to our anticipated movements, and our order of concepts reflects this spontaneous work of life. We tend to forget, however, the origin of this order and we attribute it to the world itself.

The substantiality of mind

Bergson emphasizes on various occasions that consciousness is not a thing, properly speaking, or a substance, but the movement itself of time-memory. He seems to attach importance to this distinction, which he drew as a reaction to the legacy of Descartes and Leibniz, but it is perhaps no more than the restatement of his theory of the identity of memory and consciousness. If we stick by the Aristotelian tradition and define substance, as opposed to attribute, as 'independence', or the inability to be predicated of something else (an attribute is a quality *of* something, substance is not), there is no reason why consciousness, in Bergson's sense, should not be a substance: it is not parasitic on any other object and its duration does not depend on the duration of anything else.

It is not hard to detect the source of this confusion. The concept of substance was originally modelled on the common-sense representation of compact, relatively stable

physical objects. It was an equally common-sense notion
(or according to Bergson, a notion of common sense that
was itself designed in keeping with the body's needs, and
was bound to distort the world accordingly) that the very
idea of movement implies the moving thing, therefore the
'thing' is both logically and empirically prior to any act: a
resting thing is conceivable, a movement without a moving
body is not. Bergson challenged this apparent truism. From
a disinterested, contemplative point of view – as opposed
to the normal utilitarian approach – movement is the
primitive reality, and 'things' are products of a special kind
of attention our mind pays to what is repeatable in the
world and susceptible of being included in our hierarchy of
concepts. It is of the utmost practical importance to
distinguish degrees of relative stability in perceptible
qualities; by focusing our attention on those with a higher
degree of stability we produce 'things' or 'substances'. Thus
far, Bergson was in agreement with Ernst Mach (whom he
does not mention, however). In reality, things are events
of a special kind, temporary crystallizations of images; it
would be proper to say that, for Bergson, movement is the
real and original stuff the world is made of, whereas the
picture of the universe as consisting of distinct material
objects is an artefact of intelligence. This idea – the logical
and metaphysical priority of events over objects – was to
be subsequently taken up and developed in detail by A. N.
Whitehead, probably not without inspiration from
Bergson.

The question of substantiality becomes more obscure
when we apply it to the life of the mind. Here the
distinction between 'substance' and 'movement',
whichever is considered prior, is much more remote from
common-sense considerations, and we notice the
confusion throughout the entire debate on Descartes'

Meditations (Gassendi, for instance, argued that from 'I think' Descartes infers 'I am the thinking', which, he said, is as absurd as saying 'I dance, therefore I am the dance'). And even though both the concept of spiritual substance and criticism of it had enjoyed a long tradition, it was not at all clear how to describe the distinction between consciousness which is substance and consciousness which is movement. Strictly speaking, the distinction might be intelligible on Hume's assumption that mental life is nothing but a collection of singular impressions and ideas, the conceptual crystallization of which as mind or substance is a verbal figment: the origin of the concept might be accounted for by the similarities of impressions, but it is a figment all the same; no persisting self is given in, of justifiable by, experience. In other words, the contrast between a mind which is conceived of as a thing and a mind which has been reduced to a series of events, with no 'substratum' left, is intelligible only if the former is simply annulled as a useless phantom. This is not, of course, Bergson's position: quite the contrary. The time-generating continuous self is a reality, indeed it is the first reality of which we can be certain; why then is it wrong to count it among 'things'? The reason apparently is this. The self is not only in an uninterrupted process of growth, reabsorbing and reasserting, as it were, its entire past at each moment of its present and thus producing a new 'whole' time and again. Its main characteristic is that its persistence or continous identity is no more and no less than memory. In other words, a mind without memory is inconceivable, it is a contradiction in terms, and in this sense the self is not a substance.

Memory is not a kind of spiritual space, through which I carry my continous ego; time is not an empty Newtonian flow which happens to be filled with events but has a self-dependent existence and would be there even if no events occurred. There can be no distinction between the form of memory and its actual content, between the ego and the perceptions or recollections that are put 'into' or superimposed 'on' it. I am what I remember, consciously or otherwise. It would therefore seem to make no sense to speak of continous identity in the sense of an immutable kernel which preserves itself amid changes; such metaphors are borrowed from the spatial imagination. I am new at every moment but, by including the whole of my past in my present, I remain the same person. And, if we make an effort to free ourselves from our space-related mental habits, we see that there is no contradiction between our never being identical at any two points or segments in time (to speak of points in time is already a concession to the language of geometry; there are no real points or segments in time) and being a continuous personal existence.

The question of self-identity is more difficult and has formidable consequences when God is spoken of. We shall deal with it later on.

Immortality

Personal continuity, in Bergson's eyes, has no definable limit or end. Having established, to his satisfaction, the distinction between the repository of pure recollections and cerebral memory, that is, the acquired habits or dispositions of the body, he believed there were good reasons for asserting the independence of the former from the latter and thus its ability to survive the death of the organism. Experience is incapable of proving the immortality of the soul, since no infinite duration can be conclusively inferred from experimental facts, and Bergson refused to make deductions, in the Platonic, Cartesian, or

Thomist manner, from a rationally constructed essence of the soul. The endless life of the soul can only be a matter of religious revelation. Still, he was unshakeably convinced that survival is not only possible but highly probable in the light of existing experience. The only reason why we might believe in the termination of personal existence, he argued, is the disintegration of the body. Provided that pure memory is not attached to, produced by, or preserved in, brain tissue, its continuity beyond the decomposition of our organism is a very plausible hypothesis. Bergson expressed this belief in similar terms in a number of his writings subsequent to *Matter and Memory*, though not yet in the latter work itself.

> Here is the working brain. Here is the consciousness that feels, thinks, and wills. If the work of the brain corresponded to the whole of consciousness, if there were an equivalence between the cerebral and the mental, consciousness would possibly follow the fate of the brain and death would be the end of everything; at least experience would not say anything to the contrary, and a philosopher who asserted survival would have to support his doctrine on some, usually fragile, metaphysical construction. However, if mental life, as we have tried to show, goes beyond the cerebral, if the brain is limited to translating into movements a small part of what goes on in consciousness, then survival becomes so likely that the burden of proof is on those who deny rather than those who affirm it. That we see the body disorganized is the only ground for the belief in the extinction of consciousness after death, and this ground becomes worthless if one establishes as a fact that nearly the whole of consciousness is independent of the body. (S 59)

In his last book, Bergson made the distinction between his metaphysical, or experience-based, reasons for asserting the survival of the mind, and various mythological beliefs in immortality; he also gave an explanation of the fact that nature itself prevents us from gaining absolute certainty in the matter. His belief in the mind's survival after death was never stirred by doubt. When we consider the simplicity of the transition from the independence of memory to the idea of an afterlife, we can be virtually certain that he held this belief when writing *Matter and Memory*, although for some reason he failed explicitly to state it. When he quoted, in 1904, Ravaisson's *Philosophical Last Will*, where the recently deceased philosopher expressed his firm belief in immortality and in a future encounter with departed loved ones, he did this with obvious sympathy.

He did not want to speculate on the question of how a disembodied spirit might perceive the world and what sort of perception this would be. (We should remember that he saw hypothetical pure perception as part of the images, rather than of consciousness; that in actual perception, memory is active; and that the brain is a meeting-place of matter with mind. Perhaps dream perception comes closest to what perception liberated from the supervision of the brain might be like.) He did not believe that experience had thrown enough light on such questions, although he thought that further progress could be made by examining the question of survival. His active interest in parapsychological phenomena was no doubt, at least in part, motivated by this expectation.

Comment

It does not appear that Bergson gave conclusive arguments for his theory of the independence of memory from the brain. The present author is not competent to comment on the enormous progress that neurophysiology and the study of memory have made since Bergson's day. Granted, however, that Bergson's analysis of the fallacies expressed by the psychologists of his day was justified, it is nevertheless possible, in the absence of such competence, to argue that it did not yield the results he had expected. No one nowadays believes that the brain tissue is engraved with an infinite number of separate recollections, rather like a phonographic instrument; no neurophysiologist would deny that there are many mysteries in the way in which the nervous system preserves past experiences. We must not, of course, use an argument *ex ignorantia*, in the manner of some ancient theologians. No one can say with any certainty how far and in what detail an 'equivalence' between states of consciousness and biochemical processes in the nervous substance can be established. But scientists must work on the assumption that there is no absolute limit to this inquiry. There is nothing a priori impossible in the idea that we will one day be able to depict and reconstruct, say, the content of dreams on the basis of neurophysiological and biochemical investigations, even though the technique of such an inquiry is unimaginable, and we may think that such a technique will never be available for physical reasons. In other words, a theory of perfect equivalence, albeit unprovable, is nevertheless a 'regulative idea' for scientists, and one which guides their research.

Still, no matter how far this kind of investigation could go, Bergson was probably right in insisting that 'equivalence' does not mean 'identity' and that we can always refuse to admit that what we experience is reducible to what goes on in our body; that the statement 'I feel a pain in my heart' can never *mean* the same as a description, however detailed, of the defects of my heart and of the mechanism whereby the signals of those defects are transmitted to my brain. This is, of course, a question which has been hotly debated by philosophers for centuries, and we cannot here do justice to the arguments which materialists and their opponents have advanced respectively for and against the identity theory. Suffice it to say that the debate is philosophical in the strict sense, in other words, can never be resolved by experimental research, neurophysiological or otherwise, it can never end with universal agreement, and most likely it will last until the end of the world and possibly beyond it.

In defending the independence of mind from body, Bergson seems to have been guilty of confusing two logically independent questions. It is one thing to maintain that consciousness 'goes far beyond' states of the nervous system, that the most trivial mental events are infinitely richer than the corresponding physiological processes in the sense that no 'parallelism' of both can ever be found; this Bergson failed to prove. It is another thing to argue that, whether or not it is proper to say that in conscious experience I am 'aware of the state of my body', this awareness is of an entirely different nature from, and not reducible to, those states. This distinction, of Cartesian origin, is still tenable, all the prohibitions of behaviourists notwithstanding, even if (as Bergson would readily admit) we lack the adequate language to express it in terms that would satisfy the criteria of an 'objective' description, precisely because the content of my experience can often be communicated in an intelligible way while the quality of its being experienced by me cannot be transmitted to another person. This distinction will not be abolished by any progress that might be made in investigating the equivalence between mental and organic processes, nor is it likely that it will be established by such progress. I can begin with this distinction (as Bergson and the Cartesians did), on the basis of irrefutable self-evidence, and refuse to admit that the pronoun 'I' is an ordinary common noun and that it has the same extension as the pronoun 'he' uttered by another person about myself. If this is my starting-point it *is* irrefutable, and nobody may in good faith declare it unintelligible. Whoever says that it is illicit to start with an experience which is not, by definition, 'objectifiable', cannot be refuted either. These two options are understandable, mutually exclusive, and divided by an unbridgeable gulf; once you choose one of them, no argument which you might share with your adversary will move you to switch to the other.

Nevertheless, even if I accept that my conscious experience cannot be reduced to a description of my body and that we are faced with a difference of 'essence', it does not follow, contrary to Bergson, that the mind survives the death of the body. Survival is not ruled out by experience, and arguments taken from brain physiology or from the theory of evolution can never be conclusive and can therefore be dismissed, as they used to be, as irrelevant to the question. But it is hard to imagine that any investigation of the brain could yield positive evidence for survival; and views which favour it are most likely, as in Bergson's case, to fall back on argument *ex ignorantia*.

Briefly, Bergson's description of the mind and its independence from the brain is not refuted; it is conceivable that what he said was true, but it is most doubtful that this truth could be inferred from the 'objective' data of experience which he employed to justify his beliefs.

5 Life and matter

Teleology and mechanism: the life-drive

Creative Evolution was probably the most widely read of Bergson's books. Its philosophical importance lay in the fact that it was the boldest attempt to assimilate the theory of evolution to a world view which implied a Great Mind at the steering-wheel of the universe and the absolute irreducibility of the human soul to its material conditions. In this Bergson had at least one predecessor, although there is no evidence that he had ever heard of him. Even before the publication of Darwin's work, Jakob Frohschammer, a German theologian, had argued that the human mind, through a natural evolution, had emerged from inorganic matter and that such a theory did not contradict Christian doctrine. He was to be condemned by Pope Pius IX in 1862 in the epistle 'Gravissimas Inter', less for his evolutionistic beliefs than for his preaching for the absolute freedom of thought in Church and for his rationalist manifestos; he remained, however, a believing Christian. Frohschammer's ideas had little impact outside Germany and they were discussed in a period when Darwinism had only just started to make headway in the intellectual life of Europe. Bergson's book, apart from being a literary masterpiece, appeared almost half a century after the *Origin of Species* and had to face an enormous amount of research which had been done in the mean time in support of evolutionism by biologists and palaeontologists.

For decades both adherents and enemies of Darwinism perceived in it not only a blow to the biblical story of creation but an ultimate argument for the materialist concept of man and of life: if the emergence of higher life-forms, including the human brain and mind, can be accounted for by the natural mechanisms of selection, the idea of divine providence and of the immaterial soul are – so it seemed – buried forever. There were roughly three stages in the history of the Christian response to the theory of evolution. After a period of intransigent resistance, more and more theologians were ready to admit that the theory was compatible with the Christian faith on the condition that the human species be excluded from it as having been formed by a separate act of creation. Eventually many went much further: it does not contradict Christian beliefs, they said, to admit that even man emerged from lower animal species as a result of evolution; God, however, implanted the rational soul in him once the body, which had naturally evolved, was ready to accept it.

This self-defence, though good enough to remove the logical incompatibility of transformism with the Christian tradition, was somewhat artificial: it was clearly designed to make Christianity invulnerable to the progress of biology and it awkwardly married a reluctant acceptance of the life sciences with the dogmatic supernaturalism immured in its unverifiability.

Bergson's attempt was entirely different. He espoused the theory of transformism without reluctance, even enthusiastically, although he argued that the Darwinist concepts of accidental variations and mechanical selection can account only for a tiny portion of the evolutionary process. He wanted to show that this process, although far from infallible, or planned in advance in all its details, unmistakably displays an internal purposefulness which can only be explained as the work of divine energy. He did not satisfy theologians – far from it; but his panorama of evolution provided the most efficient device for reconciling the picture of the world-in-process with the Christian notions of the human spirit and of creation. His work changed the intellectual climate in Europe: its impact was immense.

Having built his previous work on the dichotomy between mind and matter, Bergson now concentrated on the distinction between matter and life. He interpreted the human mind in terms of life energy, the latter being seen as a product of the universal spirit. We have to see cognitive acts within the general framework of life; this does not mean that all knowledge has only pragmatic value and that the question of truth in the usual sense is pointless; it does mean, however, that we ought to examine the pragmatic side of the operations of the mind. Our intelligence is at home among solid bodies and is designed to deal with them efficiently. It is therefore naturally prone to investigate the phenomena of life in the same way that it studies inert matter. The specificity of life eludes it, whereas instinct grasps life itself directly, but is unable to search for it and to express what it 'knows'. Intelligence and instinct are two different organs which nature produced to enable living creatures to cope with their environment, both organic and inorganic. Matter has a tendency to fabricate isolable systems, or 'individuals'; only in living things is this tendency properly implemented, although their individuality allows infinite gradation and fails to achieve perfection even in the highest organisms, because absolute individuality would prevent any part of an organism from living separately, and thus would make reproduction impossible.

Life, like our consciousness, is infinitely creative and inventive, incessantly producing new forms; it is a movement that must struggle with the resistance of inert matter and have recourse to all sorts of tricks in order to use matter for purposes which are foreign to it. Each new species is, as it were, a solution to a problem; there is nothing astonishing in the fact that some solutions prove to be wrong and are later abandoned. The evolutionary process teems with dead ends, failures, half-baked projects, and circuitous routes; nature proceeds somewhat gropingly, often trying several roads before it finds the right one. But it is driven constantly by an inherent tendency, and to uncover this tendency would be to understand the life of the universe.

It is very important to realize, according to Bergson, that neither the mechanistic nor the finalistic explanation of evolution is acceptable. The mechanistic view is applicable to some fragments which we artifically cut out from the world for practical purposes: it can be applied neither to the universe as a whole nor to the phenomenon of life. Yet the belief in teleology, in perfect finality, *à la* Leibniz, is simply mechanism in reverse; it implies, too, that everything is ready-made, that evolution consists in building forms designed in advance and that consequently it creates nothing. This kind of finalism destroys novelty and annihilates *time*, which would, on this assumption, serve only to unfold a programme worked out from the beginning; for both mechanists and finalists, everything is given, reality is always something made, never in the making. But, let us repeat, time is real. It turns out, in Bergson's description, to be the characteristic not only of individual human consciousness but of life as well. 'The more we focus our attention on the continuity of life, the more we see how organic evolution comes closer to the evolution of consciousness where the past presses the present to give birth to a new form which is incommensurable with its antecedents' (C 27).

On the other hand, the doctrine of vitalism, which

implies a kind of 'internal finality' inherent in each organism, is not acceptable either, both because in all species some tissues have various degrees of independence from the whole of the organism, and because the individuality of a living creature never achieves perfection. Purposefulness is an aspect of life as a whole, and not of single organisms; it does not consist in materializing pre-existing models, but in trying, albeit not always successfully, to follow a direction.

This does not, of course, entail that there is nothing but harmony in nature. Even though it is propelled by a direction-giving tendency, it can only proceed by constant diversifications, generating species and individuals who think only of their own survival and welfare, a process which results in endless struggles.

This creative tendency is the *élan vital*, or 'life-drive' – a term associated with the stereotype of 'Bergsonism' and which was to become famous. It is the original energy that, by infinite bifurcations and wrestling with the resistance of matter, produces higher and higher variations of both instinct and intelligence. Something of this original impulse is preserved in all species and all individual organisms, all of them working unconsciously in its service. The concept of the *élan vital* has been repeatedly attacked as a verbal device lacking any explanatory value, an empty 'occult quality' which, as a tool for understanding life, leaves us in exactly the same place that we were without it. To which it might be replied that the life-drive probably cannot be reforged into an empirical concept according to scientific criteria (Bergson believed it could, although he had his own ideas about what makes science), but that it is not empty in the sense that occult qualities are: it implies a kind of intentionality, however vaguely defined, in the evolutionary process, and one cannot reasonably argue that the picture of the organic process regulated only by mechanical elimination does not differ, except for terminology, from the view that the universe is steered by intention.

Life, then, is a continuous process in which the original drive divides itself into a growing variety of forms, but retains a basic direction. It has no goal, Bergson says, in the sense that human actions have goals, in other words, no one can anticipate its future course, which is more similar to an artistic creation than to the operation of a machine. The Darwinian theory of chance variations, some of which, better adjusted, happen to survive, is unacceptable for many reasons, as its critics pointed out from the very beginning. It cannot explain the similarity between life organs developed along independent lines of evolution, for instance in plants and animals; how could similar sequences of slight accidents have been repeated independently in various branches of evolution? It cannot explain complicated organs such as the eye of a vertebrate, which is functional only when fully formed, and thus the gradual acquisition of some of its elements would not have increased the chances of survival; yet on the Darwinian theory, the eye could not have appeared suddenly, fully equipped and ready to assume its function. On either hypothesis – minute variations or sudden and comprehensive changes – Darwin's doctrine would be understandable only on the assumption that a benevolent genius was helping evolution from outside. Lamarck's theory of adaptation might explain the structural analogies in divergent lines of evolution, but it implies massive hereditary transmission of acquired characteristics, whereas such heredity seems to be only a marginal phenomenon. Eimer's hypothesis of variations following a steady course would serve us better.

A hereditary change of a well-defined direction, which proceeds through accumulation and self-composition in such a way that it builds a more complex machinery, clearly has to be related to a kind of effort, but an effort which is differently profound than an individual one, differently independent of circumstances, common to most specimens of the same species and included in the germs they carry, rather in their substance, thus being able to be conveyed to their descendants. (C 88)
This effort is nothing other than the life-drive itself.

Insects and man

The life energy has to overcome the obstacles erected not only by matter but by life forms as well; the results usually turn against the principle of creativity itself, as in human efforts of expression: once produced, each form sticks to its identity and resists further changes. But the original force never sleeps. The species which focus their efforts on building defensive shelters and shells usually close the road to progress, whereas those that take greater risks and buy flexibility of movement at the price of weakened armour, prove to be winners in terms of evolution.

In the development of the animal kingdom, two main lines prove to be the most successful: the line of insects which culminates in social insects of the hymenoptera order (such as ants and bees) and the line of vertebrates, which has achieved its highest form in the human species. Man and hymenoptera represent respectively the most evolved stages of two fundamental organs of life, intelligence and instinct, and it is through their behaviour that we can best investigate the intention of nature.

Instinct and intelligence retain traces of their common origin, and we do not observe them in a perfectly pure form: the vestiges of instinct can be seen in intelligence and the halo of intelligence in instinct. The main task of intelligence is to produce artificial tools from inorganic matter, whereas instinct is a faculty for using organized instruments. The latter is strictly specialized, spontaneous, effortless and perfect; the former requires effort, mediating devices, and its results are necessarily imperfect. Nature has to choose between the two, as it cannot indefinitely intensify both abilities in the same species. Working on the assumption that only one solution is possible, instinct does not need consciousness, the latter being a measure of distance between a representation and an action, and implying a choice among various options available. In so far as they have innate 'knowledge', intelligence knows the form and instinct knows matter; intelligence assures the conscious organisms a flexibility, an ability to enlarge their knowledge indefinitely, but it limits them as well. What intelligence can conceive clearly is only what is discontinuous and immobile; what it grasps in movement is positions, rather than mobility itself. This explains the naturally 'geometrical' attitude of our minds, their essentially spatial imagination, their search for what is repeatable, abstract, and useful in manipulating solid bodies, their ineptitude in grasping what is new, and their refusal to admit creativity. Human language, that marvellous invention of nature, reflects the nature of intelligence; it may be said, conforming with Bergson's idea, that it conveys reality to us by distorting it in the process, as it tends to disregard the unique, to immobilize the mobile and artificially to dissect what is organically united. Instinct, in contrast, includes an ability to grasp life directly, in a movement of sympathy. Human beings retain a cognitive analogue of instinct: this is precisely intuition, or instinct which has become disinterested and self-aware.

Life is consciousness which has penetrated matter and

is thus compelled to make irreversible choices. In trying to 'liberate' itself, it split into two lines and found its fullest expression in the human species, which might be called the *raison d'être* of the entire organization of life on earth.

It appears that the Bergsonian philosophy is itself to be understood, as a historical phenomenon, within its conceptual framework: it is supposed to be the revindication of intuition in a world dominated by intelligence and by our naturally 'Platonic' dispositions. This philosophy does not pretend to replace the intuition or to perform its task; it can, however, help focus our attention on this universally human faculty which enables us to coincide with our own time and thereby to understand that in ourselves we touch and feel the stream of life which is coextensive with the divine consciousness.

God and nothingness

The primordial life impulse aims to expand as much as possible the realm of freedom in the world and to do this it has to wrestle incessantly with the inertia of matter, with the effects of the second principle of thermodynamics (the tendency towards thermodynamic equilibrium) which it opposes. A centre of creative energy works to defeat time and again the natural tendency towards disintegration and death. This centre is God: not a thing, but the action itself. 'Thus defined, God has nothing of the ready-made, he is uninterrupted life, action, freedom. And the creation, so conceived, is not a mystery; we experience it in ourselves when we act freely' (C 249). This is the only sentence in *Creative Evolution* where the word 'God' actually appears, and it prompts a number of questions.

God, we are told, is not a thing or a substance, but creativity itself. This is no doubt in keeping with Bergson's general beliefs that permanent 'things' reflect our relative viewpoints on the world, rather than the original reality, and that action precedes the object. The divine mind, although original and independent, is like ours in the sense that its identity consists of memory and its work involves an uncertain anticipation. God is time-bound, or rather, he is time itself, and our time mysteriously participates in his while not being a mere aspect of it. We are also free and creative; our creativity cannot simply be an instrument through which God reveals himself. Consequently, God cannot be an absolute in the sense in which the Christian God is. The absolute God is timeless, he lives in the eternal present, he does not need mediating devices like memory and anticipation; to deny this is to destroy his wholeness, his unity, and his perfect self-containment. Bergson's God may seem more comprehensible to us than the God of Christian theologians because we can imagine him as a real person, and we are unable to conceive of a personality without time. The description of an absolute, self-contained, and timeless being strongly suggests Spinoza's God, who cannot share the characteristics of a person.

In this sense it may be argued that the label 'pantheism', which Christian critics have so often tagged on to Bergson's philosophy, is unjustified: this God cannot have all his future creative work embedded eternally in his immutable essence; by creating the world he creates himself, he is as it were a living and growing God. Unlike the Christian God he faces various options instead of unfolding in time the ready-made archetypes from his spirit. He lives like each of us.

On the other hand, it seems that Bergson's God, precisely because his nature is creativity, cannot, by even the greatest effort of abstraction, be conceived of apart from the world; it simply makes no sense to talk about a self-sufficient being who subsists whether or not he 'objectifies' himself in his creatures. There is no way that the producer could be conceptually grasped as being alone, without relation to his products.

To be sure, Aquinas's God is also know to us by the intermediary of his creatures. However, in his view this is a result of our natural limitations: what we know of God we know relatively, in the mirror of his workshop, because our finite intelligence is not capable of penetrating his hidden essence; none the less we know a priori that there is no ontologically necessary link between God and the world. And yet to Bergson this link is ontological, not one which results from our cognitive ineptitude. In this sense the label 'pantheism' is not inappropriate.

Another question, much debated among Bergson's critics, concerns his 'monism'. Even on the assumption that God is not omnipotent in the traditional sense, that the future results of his creation cannot be known to him by definition, that he makes various attempts without necessarily succeeding at the first try, is he the only creator, or must he cope with a world not made by him? 'The life-drive ... cannot create absolutely', Bergson says, 'because it encounters and faces matter, that is, movement opposite to its own. But it seizes matter, which is necessity itself, and aims at putting into it the greatest possible amount of indeterminacy and freedom' (C 252). This strongly suggests that Bergson's God, like the demiurge of the Manichaeans, always finds himself in a situation beyond his control: he is compelled to fight and outwit a foreign power which is simply there.

On the other hand, Bergson says, 'it is consciousness, or rather, superconsciousness [presumably identical with God] which is at the origin of life. It is a rocket whose extinguished remnants fall in the form of matter' (C 261). This seems to imply, more in keeping with the Christian idea, that the process of creation has one source; God, however, cannot combine everything with anything and the original eruption of creative energy must begin by erecting obstacles to its further expansion: in order to organize conditions for a freedom other than his own, God had to produce matter, in which he subsequently finds an eternal foe; matter is both a condition of the movement of life and a resistance to be overcome. This seems to conform to the spirit of Bergson's philosophy.

Bergson could also probably have said that it is meaningless to ask about his 'monism' because the question amounts to asking whether there was only one or more creation *ex nihilo*. Creation *ex nihilo* never occurred, for no other reason than that *nihil* is a non-concept, an empty word. The criticism of 'nothingness' is an important ingredient of his metaphysics. It is the practical attitude of our intellect which fabricates the nonsensical idea of 'nothing'. The absence of something we expect or wish to see is the foundation on which the abstract idea of total absence, of nothingness, is built. Since we can mentally abolish any particular thing, we imagine that we can abolish the whole and think of an empty abyss replacing the universe; as a result of this imaginary trick we are led to the Leibnizian question: 'why does something exist, rather than nothing?' But the question is absurd: absence is a category relative to our recollection and anticipations, with no ontological meaning whatsoever. As Kant rightly observed, there is no difference between thinking of something and thinking of the same thing as existing; therefore to conceive of an object as not existing is to add the idea of exclusion to its representation. In fact, to deny existence is only to substitute something else in place of the object imagined, and imagining 'nothing' is simply impossible. In this sense the question 'why?' addressed to being is a pseudo-question, as is the debate concerning the absolute beginning, whether one or more creators were involved.

It should be stressed that this being about which the 'why?' cannot reasonably be asked is not a primordial substance, nor a timeless source of temporal entities: it is time itself. Once we locate ourselves within the process we realize that *durée* is the fundamental reality, whereas all the well-shaped forms are in fact our stabilizing views on an incessantly changing reality. Contrary to the tenets of Plato and Plotinus, real time is not an enfeebled eternity: the timeless being is a figment of geometrically oriented human intelligence, which works on the assumption that everything is 'given'; in reality 'time is inventiveness or nothing at all' (C 341). And it *is* nothing to modern philosophy, as we can see in the examples of Leibniz and Spinoza.

Bergson addressed himself to the pantheist interpretation of his cosmology in his two letters of 1908 and 1912 to Joseph de Tonquédec. In rebutting the criticism of the prominent French Thomist, he explained that, in his view, all energies (*élans*) come from the free activity of God, who is consequently not to be identified with the world; the impossibility of nothingness does not exclude the transcendent cause of the universe. 'Out of all this emerges clearly the idea of God, the free creator, who generates both matter and life; his creative effort continues in the realm of life, by the evolution of species and the constitution of human persons' (W 2.365). This implies the refutation of monism and pantheism.

The art of making people laugh

The contrast between life and matter is employed by

Bergson to explain various facets of aesthetic perception, especially the phenomenon of the comic. In the essay on laughter published in 1900, long before *Creative Evolution*, Bergson argues that all the varieties of objects and situations which provoke laughter – whether deliberately produced, as in comedies and jokes, or arising unintentionally in daily life – can be ultimately reduced to a type of human behaviour which displays the characteristics of mechanical movement.

> The comic is that side of a person in which he resembles a thing; it is that aspect of human events which, by a special kind of rigidity, imitates a mechanism pure and simple, an automatism, a lifeless movement. It thus expresses an individual or collective imperfection which calls for immediate correction. Laughter is this very corrective. (R 66–7)

The existence of art, Bergson argues, is to be accounted for by the fact that our perceptions are shaped by our physical needs: we organize and simplify the world according to the practical significance that its various qualities might have for us. If we communed directly with reality, if the world were perceived in its unadulterated form, art, as a special way of expressing and perceiving, would be redundant. Since our perception shapes objects according to criteria of utility, their individuality, their uniqueness, escapes us and we attend only to what is repeatable; this includes our perception of other people's and our own feelings, of which we normally retain only the impersonal, abstract side. Art is an effort, on the part of privileged souls, to get rid of this utilitarian attitude, of practically convenient abstracts, and to see things in their pristine purity, to face the world without the veil. The target of art is always something unique, even though its effects, at least in the case of great artists, are perceived in their universal validity. The art which provokes laughter is an exception to this rule: the universality lies in the work itself. This is because laughter is normally associated with emotional insensibility; the comic side of events or words is addressed only to our intelligence, not to our feelings. If we laugh at a person who, in trying to sit down on a chair, lands on the floor, this is because the flexibility and purposefulness of human acts are suddenly replaced by mechanical forces. Various human vices become ridiculous in a comedy as a result of their automatic character, their lack of elasticity, and the inability of a person to adapt himself to the human environment. Life does not repeat itself: a living person repeating himself behaves like a machine and thereby provokes laughter. A law or regulation might become comical if it is applied with a rigid consistency. A tragic hero becomes comical when he sits down in the middle of a high-flown speech: we suddenly realize that he has a body, and if body prevails over soul, the effect is similar to the contrast that emerges when a mechanism is substituted for the human body. When Molière's physician declares that it is better to die in accordance with medical rules than to be cured despite them, he makes us laugh because of professional automatism he displays. If a person gives the impression of being a thing, he is bound to become ridiculous. Repetitiveness is a favourite trick in comedies: when Molière's Harpagon, confronted with many arguments against marrying his daughter to a man she does not love, repeats obstinately 'without a dowry!', he is comical; as is Orgon, repeating his question 'and what about Tartuffe?', when informed of his wife's illness. They produce the effect of a toy in which a figure, attached to a spring, jumps out, no matter how hard we try to keep it in its place. If an apparently human act turns out to result from mechanical causes, we react with laughter. The plot in many comedies consists in the fact that the same situation occurs repeatedly in different circumstances, or is reversed. Repeatability and reversibility are the characteristics of a machine: in human actions they make us laugh. Distraction is notoriously comical because it represents the loss of human ability to adjust to changes. Virtue becomes ridiculous if it is rigid (like the misanthrope's veracity) and reveals the person's unsociability. Other examples are provided by people who are incapable of adjusting their ideas to reality: Don Quixote makes us laugh when he moulds his perceptions according to a preconceived idea and sees giants instead of windmills because it is giants that he needs.

When mechanically acting forces are inserted into a chain of human actions, they reveal the incompatibility of social and human life with the characteristics of an automaton. Laughter is a corrective reaction of the human intelligence, reason's resistance to the confusion of the human with the mechanical, a reassertion of humanity.

Comment

Bergson believed that his cosmology, like other parts of his work, was a strict extrapolation from existing experience. In this he was certainly over-optimistic, at least in the sense that his partial acceptance of finality and of the divine creation, though not contradicting experience, could not be inferred from it; this was an interpretation imposed on the data of science, yet not logically embedded in them. The present author is not in a position to discuss the validity of Bergson's strictures on Darwinist explanations; the extent to which the mechanisms of chance variation and elimination account for the evolutionary process is still a matter of dispute, and many evolutionists do not believe that the emergence of all life-forms and all organs can be sufficiently explained in Darwinian terms. But the idea of the creative *élan* and of a purposeful cosmic energy is not likely to be conclusively based on this kind of criticism, however justified; no matter how strongly we resent the picture of the organic world proceeding from protozoa to man as a result of mechanical errors in copying genetic programmes, or how persuasive we find the idea of a direction in the evolutionary Odyssey, the binding code of scientific inquiry, established in the last four centuries of our civilization, prevents us from perceiving traces of God in the machinery of matter. Many competent researchers, faced with the huge amount of facts which have been accumulated in recent decades and which are not likely to be explicable within the framework of Darwinism, are now toying, at least tentatively, with an idea of evolution that, albeit not planned, does follow a direction, and with the concept of an unknown separate principle responsible for order and form in the evolutionary process. This is perhaps closer to the Bergsonian *élan*. Yet an enormous distance separates this guesswork from a substantiated hypothesis of a superconsciousness, let alone divine consciousness, paving the way, however erratically, for the ultimate triumph of the spirit. Of course, the code of science is a human work, a collection of human decisions, and it can therefore be changed. Many philosophers have been working to change it, and Bergson was one of them. The rules of scientific empiricism are not themselves a logical product of empirical investigation and may be defied. Yet if we try to enlarge the concept of science in Bergson's manner and show that on this latitudinarian definition science can support the panoramic view of the universe suggested by his cosmogony and cosmology, this will probably not be science in the strict modern sense. We can therefore make a remark analogous to what has been said about Bergson's theory of mind and body. Bergson's metaphysics may conceivably be true; no experience can convince us beyond doubt that there is no divine energy at work in evolution, no intention which leads the world in a well-defined direction. Keeping to the rigours of scientific inquiry, we may say: perhaps the universe really *does* move in the way Bergson thought it did, perhaps it is under the guidance of a creative and loving Person; but we cannot positively reinforce this belief by scientific examination, unless we alter the rules of what is or is not accepted by scientific standards.

The central idea of Bergson's cosmology is this: the Whole is of the same nature as myself. The time-generating life of the consciousness is the model for the universe. Our inner experience of time is the most irresistible fact we encounter. We should start with the real stream of conscious life, after dispensing with the 'geometrical' prejudices of psychology and physics (Bergson's is not a psychological approach: psychology is a natural science which has taken its rules from more developed areas and is bound to objectify the mind and to impose on it the abstract figment of physical time, a derivative of spatial imagination). How do I perform this leap from myself to the universe? By intuition, presumably, by trying to coincide with the great pulse of life. Intuition, however, admittedly cannot have equivalents in the analytical effort and is not properly translatable into rational categories. Perhaps it delivers us truth, after all, but if so, its truth is beyond the scope of language. It is in keeping with Bergson's philosophy to say that our Platonic prejudices have deeper roots than the restrictions of modern science: they are inherent in language itself. Our language is of course historically relative: no word may claim to reflect the world as it is in itself; but it is the tool we have at our disposal. It is therefore unlikely that it could reach absolute reality, divine or otherwise.

6 Society and religious beliefs

The closed and the open society

A quarter of a century elapsed between the publication of *Creative Evolution* and Bergson's next, and last, major work, *Two Sources of Morality and Religion*. Over those years he wrote a few philosophical essays, most of them continuing the themes of *Matter and Memory* and *The Essay*; he became a public figure and the beneficiary of various honours, including the Nobel Prize for Literature; he contributed to the First World War by taking diplomatic missions to the United States and Spain and by publishing a number of patriotic ('jingoistic' would perhaps be a more suitable adjective) texts. He was active, after the conclusion of peace, in international bodies and in French educational reform. He ventured into discussion with Einstein, which resulted in the publication of *Durée et simultanéité* (1922), a book he later refused to allow to be reprinted, admitting that his mathematical knowledge had not been up to the task. There was little in his public activity to reveal his major philosophical preoccupation during this period: the meaning of religion as a social phenomenon on the one hand and, on the other, as a channel through which man comes into contact with the divine.

We may notice in retrospect a similarity of polemical intention in Bergson's main works. In *Matter and Memory* he attempted to show that modern neurophysiological research did not affect the notion of the mind's independence from the organism. The goal of *Creative Evolution* was to prove that the theory of transformism, far from justifying a purely naturalistic concept of man and the universe, provided more reasons for perceiving the Great Mind behind the physical machinery. The task of *Two Sources* was to demonstrate that sociological investigations of religious phenomena and their social functions are not only compatible with, but indeed support, a view of religious life as a form of communication with the original *élan* which penetrates the world and coincides with the spirit of the Creator. Throughout these works Bergson tried to assimilate into his spiritualist outlook those tenets of modern science which had seemingly established the materialistic doctrine and done away forever with the religious legacy of mankind; he sought to reveal that we do not need to question anything in the genuine body of science in order to question its materialist interpretation. The latter, far from being a logical consequence of empirical research, is a philosophical prejudice arbitrarily imposed on facts; once we reduce new scientific discoveries to their proper content, we shall see that the materialist reduction of God, mind, and religion to physical, psychological, and social realities is itself a mental bias which we have inherited from the old mechanistic metaphysics.

Thus, after neurophysiology and biology, social anthropology became the object of Bergson's critical assimilation. Anthropological inquiry into the sources and function of forms of religious life had evolved, in Bergson's lifetime, into a relatively autonomous discipline, to which a number of outstanding minds had contributed, and which, of course, teemed with sharp controversies. Durkheim's *Les formes élémentaires de la vie religieuse (Elementary Forms of Religious Life)* (1912), was, along with a number of his minor works, one of the most influential books on the subject and the one, no doubt, with which Bergson was most familiar. There are few direct polemics in *Two*

Sources and very few footnotes (Durkheim is mentioned twice, occasionally we find the names of Lévy-Bruhl, Mauss, Westermarck; there are no references to British or American anthropologists), yet clearly his former colleague from the École Normale was the main target of his criticism. Durkheim directly answered the question, 'what are religious beliefs for?', by invoking the collective consciousness and the need for a society to project social bonds and various structures of communal life onto a mythological imagery. Bergson's work is not properly speaking anthropological; it is rather a philosophical examination of anthropological material.

The main opposition on which *Two Sources* rests is not that of society/religion or morality/religion; it is rather the contrast between purely social, and socially explicable, forms of both religious and moral life (closed society, static religion) and their higher, qualitatively different manifestations (open society, dynamic religion) in which we perceive the collaboration of the human mind and imagination with the creative source of Being. The acts *par excellence* of this coalescence are performed by the great mystics. Bergson for many years had been interested in mystical phenomena; in 1909 he reviewed a book by Henri Delacroix on the history and psychology of mysticism, which probably initiated him into the spiritual world of St Teresa and Madame Guyon.

The moral obligations we obey, or at least pretend to obey, (if we merely pretend, this proves, of course, that we feel their pressure even if we try to evade it) are, Bergson says, the work of nature. In a society which, unlike the anthill, consists of free individuals, each of them capable of abiding by or defying social norms, the system of moral rules fulfils the function which instinct alone can assure among social insects. Moral law is perceived as an order of nature – it prevents society from falling apart and it is obviously necessary for guaranteeing social cohesion. It persists in the social ego, a part of our consciousness which is impersonal but none the less makes up an aspect of ourselves. Thus when we fail to conform to its orders, we feel separated not only from other people but from ourselves as well. When a criminal voluntarily confesses his crime, it is because he feels that he is no longer the same person that other people, unaware of his past, address; by confessing and being punished he is reintegrated into society and thereby becomes himself again.

The 'obligations' which instinct imposes on ants are precise and detailed; in human communities the very presence of rules is a natural necessity, whereas their content changes from one society to another. It contributes to the health of social life that even absurd rules should be obeyed. Once nature succeeded in producing, along with the arthropods, whose social instincts are perfect, a species consisting of free and intelligent individuals – imperfect, yet capable of indefinite progress – it invented a system of coercion meant to fulfil similar functions through the intermediary of internalized habits. Moral customs and beliefs may be compared to language: all the specific characteristics of a language originate in usage, yet the faculty of speech is given by nature.

The natural system of obligations is designed to serve the particular society in which it is binding; this society, however large, is closed, that is, its constitution and self-awareness imply that its norms do not extend beyond it. There is nothing more in the plans of nature. Primitive social instinct secures cohesion for the community and opposes it to other groups; natural social bonds are formed against foreign societies and resulting war is a work of nature, as is property, which is at the root of wars. There is, furthermore, no natural transition from the tribal to the universal human morality. 'Between a nation, no matter how great, and mankind, there is a distance from the finite to the infinite, from the closed to the open' (T 27). It is impossible to enlarge the former step by step and to arrive at the latter. The leap to a morality which embraces the entire human race cannot be performed without religious inspiration.

It is only through God and in God that religion invites man to love humankind, just as it is only through reason and in reason that we all live in communion; through and in reason philosophers let us see humanity, show us the eminent dignity of the human person and everyone's right to others' respect. In neither case do we reach humanity by stages, passing through the family and the nation. (T 28)

This march towards an open society in which we are able to see humanity in everyone, and where all are equal in moral obligations and claims, was initiated in various civilizations: Greek sages, Jewish prophets, Buddhist and Christian saints have paved the way towards a universally human morality. Unlike nature, these great spirits do not command or exert pressure. They appeal to all, they find followers, and thus they prove that in our soul there is a potential force, however embryonic, that goes beyond the tribal mentality towards human fraternity. The closed soul can evolve into an open one – not by broadening its field of bonds with other people, but by acquiring another, truly human nature. It takes a creative emotion to open oneself to mankind and to abandon the way of life in which we are capable of loving some people only by hating others.

If the closed and open moralities differ from each other

in essence, rather than in degree, this is because of their in-spiring forces and because of their potential. The former is a product of natural evolution, the latter arises from religious sources; the former is made to conserve society, the latter implies an idea of progress whose carriers are the great teachers and prophets of mankind. The fomer can be explained by the natural needs of a society, the latter reaches the principle which explains the society itself, as well as the universe: the original divine energy. The guiding spirits of mankind cannot, of course, miraculously convert it into an open society, free of hatred and struggle; but their toil is not in vain. They are instruments of progress which, however slow and however hampered by the refractoriness of our tribal nature, brings us closer to a fraternal community.

The place of Christianity in this process is indeed privileged. The Platonic theory of ideas virtually implies a belief in the equal value of all human beings, but it fails to make the step from the implicit to the explicit. The sublime moral doctrines of ancient China were not designed to serve the whole of mankind. The stoics preached fraternity only as an ideal. Christianity was the first to give real force to the idea of universal brotherhood, implying the equality of humans. The way to the recognition of human rights, long and painful as it might have been historically, had been opened by the Gospels.

Both kinds of morality owe their efficacy not to their doc-trinal truth but to the emotions. Natural obligations belong to the lower, 'infra-intellectual' realm of our soul, whereas the potential for an open morality dwells in the 'supra-intellectual' area; our intelligence is located in between. It cannot fight alone against passions and self-interest; in vain do we try to shape a viable morality based on reason. Even though 'metaphysics and morality express the same thing, the former in terms of intelligence, the latter in terms of will' (T 46), intelligence cannot transform itself into an act of will and cannot enable us to obey obligations, whether they come from social pressures or from a love-drive. Ultimately, both sources of obligations must be seen as two outflows of the same energy of life; in this sense their essence is biological. The morality of pressure which keeps social bonds alive was a necessary condition of and the foundation for the universal morality of spiritual aspiration, just as matter was a condition of life. In both cases, the higher forms have to overcome the resistance of the lower stratum which has made them possible. It seems as if God, in order to shape the better part of creation, had to begin with erecting obstacles to his work. In this sense, Bergson's metaphysics continues the insight of the Christian Neoplatonists: only by alienating himself, projecting himself, so to speak, into the world and then reabsorbing it, can God arrive at the fullness of his existence.

Tribal religion

We see an analogous scheme at work in Bergson's analysis of two kinds of religion, mutually irreducible. The *static religion*, like the closed morality, is an organ devised by nature for a community of creatures endowed with the gift of thought and free choice. We are often struck by absurdities or cruelties we find in various mythologies and rituals of primitive religion. We do not need to suppose, like Lévy-Bruhl, that the people of those societies had a fundamentally different mentality or, like Durkheim, that their collective consciousness was essentially different from ours. We ought instead to look into the natural function of religious beliefs and customs. The basic function of religion is fable-generating (*fonction fabulatrice*); it has to counteract and check the socially destructive work of intelligence. A bee, having no intelligence, does not need superstitions either, whereas both are given jointly to man, because the former alone, without being limited by the latter, would disintegrate social and individual life. Mythological imagery is a substitute for instinct in human communities: it ensures stability and order. Intelligence and sociability are both of biological origin and they ultimately serve the same purpose. But without a permanent tension between them, the human species could not proceed along the path of its destiny.

First, there is nothing in our intelligence to prevent us from thinking exclusively of our own interest; intelligence encourages selfishness. Nature has invented various mythical figments – gods who protect, threaten, and punish – to defend the social order against this nefarious impact of intelligence, and religious myths never make a neat distinction between a physical and a moral order. This kind of primitive perception has by no means evaporated from the modern consciousness: 'Let us scratch the surface, erase what comes from education, and we find in ourselves primitive mankind' (T 132). We continue to feel that moral interdictions are carried by the very things they refer to.

Secondly, mythologies provide humans with a means of counteracting the discouraging power of our knowledge of the inevitability of death. For an animal this knowledge is useless, indeed harmful, but nature could not grant us the gift of reason without making us aware that we have to die. All the myths of survival emerge in reaction to this morbid wisdom. Since society is built into individual minds, it is important, if collective authority is to work, that individuals should persist in a shadowy shape after death.

Thirdly, human intelligence fills the mental space

between our objectives and our acts; unlike animals, which do not experience hesitation, we anticipate situations to which we are going to react, confront intentions with means, and realize the uncertainty of our efforts. In order to neutralize the discouraging effects of the awareness of our weakness in dealing with the world, nature has armed us with the images of intentionally friendly or hostile powers which operate within the natural chains of causes; their actions explain our failures. We replace incomprehensible accidents or mechanical causes with the figments of good or malicious powers which work in a way similar to ours and are thus less mysterious, more likely to listen to us. Thus we populate the world with all kinds of entities which, even if malevolent, are less terrifying than the blind forces of chance; they are just enemies, and can be fought against and defeated like human foes. Magic is a system of dealing with and taming the powers of chance by endowing them with human-like intentionality.

Far from being an inferior kind of science, magic is an aspect of natural religion, a part of the instinctive barrier which life erects in order to prevent our intelligence from enfeebling or dissolving men's will to assert themselves in a hostile environment. The growth of knowledge and technical skills gradually reduces, though never abolishes, the margin of uncertainty in our practical efforts, thereby correspondingly reducing our need to discover conscious intentions behind all the events and to cope with the world by magical means. Without magic the intelligence of primitive man would have paralysed his practical efforts and killed progress.

Universal religion: mysticism

Bergson's notion of static religion may appear to fall within the rationalist approach, except for the language of final causes attributed to nature: religion seems to be functionally explainable by the need for biological survival. But the emergence of 'dynamic religion' throws a new light on the meaning of the static type.

While closed morality and static religion are forces of conservation, dynamic religion is the main organ through which life assures progress both for individuals and for the human race as a whole. Since man is the *raison d'être* of the universe, and since it is through his development that free creative energy should successfully arrive at fulfilment, dynamic religion may be said to be the highest expression of the divine *élan*. Through the religious efforts of great mystics mankind goes back to the very source of Being.

Genuine mysticism, the guiding force of dynamic religion, appears very infrequently in the history of religion; but it is able to move a real, if hidden, layer in our minds and gradually transform or ennoble conservative religion which, by imitating some of its forms, eventually assimilates the essence. Thus there is progress in religious life; the transition from worshipping spirits to worshipping personal gods is already an important step forward. The power of mystical experience gives new colour to the established mythologies; no static religion is the same again after an encounter with a great mystical soul. Mysticism culminates in 'a contact, and therefore a partial coincidence, with the creative effort that life reveals. This effort is of God, if not God himself. A great mystic would be an individual going beyond the limits which have been marked out for the species by its very materiality and thereby continuing and extending the divine action' (T 233). The Greek mysticism which fertilized rationalist philosophy, survived in it, and eventually enabled it, in Neoplatonic thought, to transcend reason, failed to reach the highest stage, in which contemplation and action converge. Plotinus remained faithful to the ancient intellectualism when he perceived action as a weakened contemplation. Hindu and Buddhist mysticism, despite their sublime achievements, failed to reach the complete form. They sought a way of escaping from life and from the will to create; they did not prove capable of stimulating the effort of intelligence and technical progress, and lacked the warmth of love. In all these aspects they differed from Christianity, where the mystical impetus culminates.

In Christian mysticism contemplation and action do not collide with each other; great Christian mystics like St Paul, St Teresa, St Catherine of Siena, St Francis, and Joan of Arc radiated an extraordinary vitality inspired by love. Mystical union becomes complete when it embraces not only thought and the sentiments but the will too. Mystical love is more than human love of God, it is God's love for all humans. A great mystic loves mankind with a divine love. This love is the work neither of reason nor of the senses; it is the life-drive manifesting itself through those privileged souls and attempting to reach the entire human race. There is a tension, naturally, between the human technical effort and mystical religiosity, and it is inevitable until 'a profound change in the material conditions imposed by nature on mankind makes a radical spiritual transformation possible' (T 250). Ordinary religious life preserves something of the ardour of mysticism, but the requirements of material existence tone it down, as it were. Through these ordinary forms a little of the mystical fire can be distributed among all. The invisible pressure of great mystics survives and is reinforced when a new exceptional soul appears in due course. And even the greatest Christian mystics are imitators – original yet incomplete – of the one who stood at the origin of Christianity: Jesus Christ himself.

The God of all religions, unlike the God of Aristotle, is a Being with which we can communicate. For mystics, love is not a divine attribute, it is God himself. And he needs us, they insist, for the same reasons we need him: he needs us to love us.

Even though the certitude of the mystical experience cannot be simply converted into philosophical wisdom, the mystics, who, strictly speaking, have no problems to solve, have changed the philosophical perspective and contributed to the way philosophers ask and answer their problems: we cannot philosophize about God, love, nothingness, and creation without reference to their experience. And the most reliable method of philosophy is to look first at experience instead of concocting concepts by which reality is to be measured. Philosophers have tended to construct an idea of God and deduce from it the characteristics of the world as it should be if God existed; then, failing to perceive these characteristics, they conclude that God does not exist. In particular this is how philosophers dealt with the terrible question of evil and suffering. We speak of divine omnipotence as if we really had the idea of 'everything', including all possibilities. But this idea is as empty as that of nothingness. We cannot use it to infer from omnipotence the doctrine that God could have manufactured a world free from suffering and evil. Bergson does not attempt a theodicy, but rather points out that, strictly speaking, there is no 'problem of theodicy' as we lack the concepts to phrase it. Nevertheless he makes a profession of optimism: it is a fact that people's judgement of life as a whole is positive, because mankind clings to life; and it is a fact that there is such a thing as unmixed joy, beyond pleasure and pain: this is the mystic's experience.

Such experience also throws light on the question of survival. We cannot yet be sure whether immortality, which appears highly probable on the basis of research on memory, is of the same kind that mystics directly experience when they participate in the divine essence without their personality being dissolved or absorbed; further inquiry might clarify the issue. On the other hand, Bergson remarks, if we were absolutely sure of immortality, we would not be able to think of anything else and all our earthly pleasures would fade. Perhaps (although Bergson does not say this in so many words) uncertainty about survival after death should be seen as one of the many devices nature employs to sustain the sources of vitality and progress in human societies.

If some quasi-mystical or perhaps even truly mystical states of mind can be induced by chemical means or as a result of brain injuries, this is quite in keeping, Bergson believes, with his interpretation of the mind-body relationship. It is conceivable that some physiological disturbances caused by external or internal factors bring into consciousness those forces of the soul which lie inactive or unconscious, silenced by the brain, which, being essentially an organ of the body, filters the resources of memory and acts of perception, as well as the spiritual abilities of man, according to the body's needs. The jolting of certain inhibiting functions of the brain might activate or carry to the surface those hidden mental powers. And it should be recalled that only in great mystics, according to Bergson, is the tension between contemplation and action abolished.

In keeping with his general optismistic mood, Bergson

believed that it was the destiny of mankind to move closer and closer to the 'open society' in which wars will have been done away with, and where democratic values and respect for human rights would prevail. All progress so far had taken place amid tensions, oscillating between complementary values which mankind needs but which it could never have implemented jointly to their full extent. He believed it quite likely that a yearning after a simpler life would return, that we would prove capable of getting rid of artificial needs and that, at the same time, technical and social progress would remove the material obstacles and hardship which prevented people from directing more of their energy to spiritual advancement. There is no essential conflict between technical and scientific developments on the one hand and religious needs on the other: quite the contrary, it was material dissatisfactions and scarcities which left to us little room for the expansion of our religious needs.

Summary

As we have seen, Bergson's philosophy of history is based on the idea of discontinuous progress. His panorama of the human past is essentially heroic: it is great heroes, thinkers, geniuses, saints, and prophets who mark the points of discontinuity, the leaps which push humanity towards a better society, a better life, and a better understanding of itself and of the universe. Like the evolution of life as a whole, the evolution of man is strewn with moments of regression, dead ends, false steps, hesitations, and stagnation. Viewed as a whole, it is progress all the same.

The distinction between a closed and an open society,

static and dynamic religion is therefore, like some of Bergson's other dichotomies, less sharp than it appears at first sight. The difference, he insists, is one of nature, not of degree. However, static forms of religiosity preserve both a mystical potential and the traces of the spiritual force once implanted in them by religious geniuses; the ideas and feelings which lead the human race to an open society make progress, by inches, within tribal communities. Christianity itself cannot be spoken of as a unique and wholly open religion, as opposed to pagan cults; it is historically privileged, no doubt, but it is the perfect seat of the dynamic spirit, rather than its complete embodiment.

It has been mentioned that Bergson, according to his wife's report, felt in the last period of his life that nothing separated him from Catholicism and that he refrained from baptism because he wanted to show solidarity with the persecuted Jews. Raissa Maritain, wife of Jacques Maritain, stated, however, that he had received baptism secretly, even though she was unable to give the date of this event. If so, he must have concealed his formal conversion from his wife. George Cattaui, himself an Egyptian Jew converted to Catholicism, reports that Bergson, as it appeared from a conversation he had had with him, believed in the divinity of Jesus and in the efficacy of sacraments. We shall presently discuss Catholic reactions to Bergson's philosophy.

It is, I believe, a plausible assumption that there is a difference of essence between a tribal and a universal human morality, and the same can be said about the difference between tribal and universal religions. Furthermore, I would not deny that mystical experience is of crucial importance in religious history and that its philosophical meaning is certainly a matter for exploration.

As for Bergson's subsequent interpretations of mysticism as a manifestation of the primordial divine energy, it results from a philosophical or religious choice and cannot be derived conclusively from historical inquiry. Let us repeat the remark we made about other areas of Bergson's metaphysics: his beliefs may be true, but cannot be justified without an act of faith, on the basis of material examined according to the rules of historical research. Bergson himself repeatedly insisted on the empirical character of his investigations, but his notion of experience was much larger than the analytical rigours of modern science allow (he was well aware, of course, of this difference and distinguished science from scientism). Both the inexpressible experience of time, which everyone is capable of, and the rare experience of mystics, are included in the stuff Bergson's metaphysics is made of. He believed, too, that there was no reason why the concept of experience should be restricted in a way that experimental science recommends for its purposes. One might argue that there are indeed no transcendental reasons for such restrictions; their real reason is that they delineate the field in which people can, by using similar methods and the same logical framework, come to an agreement, whereas such agreement cannot be obtained in areas which are opened up if the notion of experience is thus enlarged. But this argument, if reasonable, implies that what matters in these restrictions is consensus and efficacy of knowledge, rather than truth. And there is no reason why people should be prevented from seeking truth wherever they hope to find it, apart from consensus and efficacy.

7 Critics and followers

Rationalist criticism: Julien Benda

Like all influential and original thinkers, Bergson was a target of numerous attacks, especially after the publication of *Creative Evolution*. The attacks came mainly from two opposing camps. For the rationalists, his philosophy amounted to the degradation of analytical reason; it attempted to replace the rigours of science by quasi-mystical insights. The orthodox Thomists attacked his alleged pantheism and nominalism and above all saw him (quite rightly) as a great ally, if not the strongest philosophical exponent, of Catholic modernism, the dreadful disease which spread throughout the Roman Catholic Church in most European countries.

The most intransigent of Bergson's foes among French rationalists was without doubt Julien Benda. In two successive books (*Le Bergsonisme, ou une philosophie de mobilité* (1912) and *Une Philosophie pathétique* (1913)) and in a number of articles, he denounced Bergsonism, from the standpoint of the Cartesian tradition, not only as a philosophy that was simply wrong, but as a glaring symptom of the general cultural degradation. In his eyes it was a barbarous appeal to passive emotions which were supposed to replace discursive thinking and offer us a higher, through unverifiable and inapplicable, insight into absolute reality. It was incapable, in spite of all Bergson's claims, of working out a 'method' or of yielding any results. Scientists like Spencer, one of Bergson's main targets, indeed failed to apprehend the movement of evolution in itself, the 'substance' of movement, but then they had never pretended to be able to arrive at this kind of impossible knowledge. The fault of intelligence, Bergson argues, is its inability to explain mobility; granted, but neither does it explain immobility or even try to do so, since the kind of explanation Bergson claims to have found is a chimeric task, a sterile hunting for the absolute which by definition cannot be an object of knowledge, whatever Bergson and William James may imagine. 'Does Bergson's work want to be life or reflection about life? An imitation of life or rather its explanation?' (*Le Bergsonisme*, p. 45). Bergson blames scientists for the 'mania of cramming facts into pre-existent categories', but it was this mania which allowed Newton to discover that planets move according to the same laws as the fall of a stone, Lavoisier to establish that respiration is a form of combustion, and Maxwell to find out that luminous vibration is dielectric polarization. Bergson sneers at knowledge and language – hoping to eliminate them in favour of an intuition which is a variety of instinct. In his 'philosophical will' we find a 'deep hatred of identity, and abhorrence of the idea that a thing may be that thing for however short a time, a passion for mobility, more exactly for contradiction, for indetermination, for the notion that a thing is that thing and at the same time something else' (ibid., p. 131).

Yet, Benda argues, Bergsonism is precisely the philosophy of our time; it flatters the fashions and the prevailing tendencies of the age, an age of hatred for science, intelligence, and intellectual effort, including philosophy in so far as it constructs abstract concepts instead of promising us an entrance into 'immediacy'. A certain amount of hatred for knowledge has always existed – did not the mob occasionally murder philosophers in antiquity? – but it has become *the* distinguishing work of our age; the predominance of the feminine, passive element can be seen in all areas of civilization, including art. Ignorant people think that science ought to provide them with absolute certainty and blame it for failing to do so; it is Bergson who deludes them into the belief that science has broken its promises and offers them instead a way of grasping the 'essence' of things in emotional acts. Benda's point seems simply to be that knowledge is by definition conceptual, and that to do away with abstract concepts amounts to barring all possible ways to knowledge. 'One can well understand, however, that a philosophy which has decided to say something will abandon the object whose essential feature is that one will be never be able to say anything about it' (*Une Philosophie pathétique*, p. 28). Bergson instructs us how we should immerse ourselves in the unknowable, and asserts that this is how we achieve a better and loftier knowledge. Philosophy is not supposed to be coherent, to offer definitions, to reason; it scorns rigour and logic; it should be a literary *genre*, an amusement, rather than a search for truth. Philosophy becomes a device to produce a thrill, to commune directly with things in quasi-sexual intimacy, to abandon ideas and arguments. In fact, Bergson accuses philosophy of not being poetry. He respects only what is singular, unique, and thus a possible source of impressions; he despises everything general, abstract, and expressible in numbers. He preaches the worship of pure 'becoming', of movement, and he would have us believe that each of us, by looking more closely into himself, can touch the principle of Being and that this principle is of the same nature as our passions. Any conceptual analysis of consciousness seems to be an attempt on our inner life.

This praise of ecstatic femininity, of instability, of pure action, this supposed liberation from language, from logic, from everything that is common and social, is the mark of a post-revolutionary civilization in which philosophy, having abandoned intellectual discipline and effort, has become a popular toy and still pretends to be a science in a more sublime sense. Cartesianism, with its cult of reason, was a philosophy of the aristocracy, whereas Bergsonism expresses the spirit of democracy which needs nothing but emotions.

Benda's hostile strictures, although unjust on some points, are not entirely unfounded. They are unjust inasmuch as Bergson never suggested that it was the calling of intuition to replace science and intelligence. Both in his books and in his rejoinders to critics like A. Binet and E. Borel (he never polemicized with Benda) he expressed the belief that mathematics and physics themselves can eventually touch the absolute, and that metaphysics, which appeals to intuition, cannot take over their tasks. Physical and chemical analysis is not capable of grasping the nature of life and consciousness, but this does not mean that their effort in those fields is illegitimate; it only means that in order to understand what is specific and essential to the phenomena of life and consciousness, we cannot be satisfied with what the experimental sciences have to offer; we have to use the 'sense of life' which is rooted in the same vital energy as instinct and it is the task of philosophy to explore and exploit this experience.

If Bergson can thus be exonerated from some of Benda's charges, he is guilty of a confusion which justifies the suspicions voiced by rationalist critics. He claimed that philosophy was not only a science ('a relative science of the absolute, a human science of the divine', as he put it in his review of a book by Janet in 1897) but, compared to all the experimental and mathematical sciences, a knowledge of a higher order basing its results on a special holistic experience which, while dispensing with linguistic 'symbols', can nevertheless be expressed in a theoretical construction; the certainty we gain through this kind of knowledge surpasses everything we find in the sciences, as they do not go beyond immobile pictures and reach reality according to ready-made conceptual categories. In other words, Bergson was not satisfied with simply describing two ways in which we assimilate reality, but made value judgements about their respective virtues. There is no compelling reason, as we have said before, that the term 'knowledge' should be reserved for propositional knowledge only, why we should forbear from attributing a cognitive value to emotions and to the 'qualitative' aspects of perception, that the experience of mystics should be despised a priori as a childish illusion and that the intelligibility must be co-extensive with the scope of rules which operate in modern science. But Bergson goes further than this. For him metaphysics, rooted in intuitive experience, grasps the whole, the essence, the soul of things; analytical inquiry, meanwhile, is bound to be content with the relative and static aspects which it cuts out of the stream of reality according to utilitarian criteria, as they are codified in our conceptual apparatus. Since whoever possesses the whole possesses also the part, it appears natural to conclude from this comparison that the results we obtain from intuitive experience embrace everything that matters, and it is not quite clear why we should need analytical knowledge as well. In other words, Bergson seems to suggest that metaphysics makes the sciences dispensable, all his protestations notwithstanding. The ambiguity of this point gives some plausibility to the attacks of rationalist critics like Benda and Russell, in spite of their ideological bias, hostility, and sometimes caricatured presentation of the doctrine we are examining.

It is likely that Bergson's anti-rationalism carries a hidden anti-technological tendency, although he never made it explicit in ideological terms (on the contrary, we have seen that he included technological development in his general speculation on mankind's spiritual progress). The point is that what Bergson believed to be the creative will might better be described as the will to be passive; he encourages us to submit to the undulations of 'life', rather than to dominate it. It is indeed clear that the human species could become 'master and possessor of nature' by unfolding and increasing the analytical power of the mind, by using abstractions and numbers. It is not in rapture over life, or in attempts to coincide with the divine energy, that the human 'will to power' over nature is expressed; it is rather in abstraction and calculation, in analysis, in the refusal to accept the world as it is, in its wholeness and oneness. Technological progress did not result from fascination with the unity of the universe but from the human effort to dissect the world into as many aspects as possible and to make them as quantifiable as possible. No doubt, much is lost in a mind which leaves no room for anything else. But it seems more reasonable to admit inescapable conflicts and tensions between various human aspirations and potentialities rather than to expect their unspoiled harmony.

Catholic critics: Maritain

Virtually all prominent Thomist philosophers in France – Maritian, Garrigou-Lagrange, Sertillanges, de Tonquédec – considered it their duty to engage in combat with the Bergsonian doctrine. It was clear that Bergson's work had created a new situation in intellectual

life. Philosophers, whether sympathizers or enemies, had
to define themselves in terms which the 'New Philosophy'
dictated. In some points, the Thomists joined the
rationalist critics: the spread of Bergsonian 'anti-
intellectualism' and contempt for reason seemed
dangerous not only to their specific metaphysical tenets but
to the Catholic faith as well. But they differed from each
other in the degree of their intransigence. More than others,
Sertillange was inclined to 'baptize' the pagan doctrine and
to admit that its energy might be usefully directed to the
cause of Christianity. He asserted that the condemnation
of 1914 was justified, as the ultimate results of Bergsonian
thought could not yet be known; *Two Sources*, however,
had revealed its Christian inspiration. After Bergson's
death Sertillage called him 'an apologist from without'; by
fighting against materialist dogmas, by arguing for freedom
and for the ontological independence of consciousness, by
revealing creativity in the evolutionary process, by
dismissing attempts to interpret morality purely in social
terms, and by seeing in Jesus Christ the culminating point
of the history of religion, Bergson repeated the work of John
the Baptist; he paved the path to the Lord.

Maritain was not inclined to make such concessions. In
the preface to the 1947 edition of his main anti-Bergsonian
work (*La Philosophie bergsonienne*) of 1913 he welcomed
Two Sources, in which, he asserted, Bergson had gone
beyond his earlier ideas, but he still considered the previous
criticism perfectly justified.

This criticism extends to all aspects of Bergson's opus.
It is, according to Maritain, a philosophy void of essences
(*désessenciée*), deliberately doing away with all
counterparts which our ideas might have in reality and
thereby with the very notion of Being. Bergson, like Kant,
regarded abstract concepts as empty forms: though not a

94

priori patterns of sensibility, they are practical attitudes of the *homo faber*, rather than instruments which give us access to reality. As a result, human intelligence becomes naturally mechanistic, as in Taine's doctrine, and our intellectual life has to be interpreted in materialistic terms. The escape from materialism is supposed to be provided by acts of intuition, which go beyond intelligence and which plunge us into the pure 'concrete'. Consequently, no rational metaphysics is possible. Bergsonian intuition, being a variety of instinct, is in fact inferior to intelligence, and thus both are degraded. Genuine intuition, as described in Thomist categories, is an intellectual act, an understanding of Being which, though not perceived, is inherent in the perceived reality; by surrendering the intellect to matter, Bergson disgraces human nature and falls prey to the Manichaean error; our contact with spiritual reality becomes anti-natural and anti-intellectual because it is void of concepts. In this Bergson follows the Buddhist tradition he assimilated through Plotinus. While his unquestionable merit was to free biology from the fetters of mechanism and to prove the irreducibility of life, he replaced cognitive acts by the sheer fact of living.

Another fundamental flaw of Bergsonian metaphysics is its failure to make a proper distinction between potentiality and actuality, or to admit the reality of either. For Bergson, time itself is creative: there is no potentiality which comes to fruition in time. What we call possible becomes so only after the event, as a result of our comprehension of the process; the possible does not precede the actual. Consequently, everything is *in actu*; things at any given moment are everything they can be. This is consistent, of course, with Bergson's complete dismissal of substance. 'To be' is replaced by 'to change': change is the primordial and original reality. The distinction between necessary and contingent vanishes as well; change is self-supporting, and all contingent events are their own causes. Therefore, whatever Bergson's intentions, no real and essential distinction between God and the world can be conceptually expressed, and God can be described only in pantheistic terms. God is a centre of continuous creative energy; we reach him by the same act of intuition that we perform when we immerse ourselves in a finite object; indeed the divine *esse* differs from the *esse* of things only by degree. Acts of creation can only be expansions of God himself, and what we in fact deal with is a creation without the creator. And since, for Bergson, nothingness is a meaningless word, creation *ex nihilo* is inconceivable by definition. Creativity, divine or human, is reduced to pure spontaneity, void of reasons. In this process there is nothing stable, no substantial unity, not even truth: intelligence is a practical device fabricated by evolution, and so its work can be assessed only in utilitarian, not in cognitive terms.

It is clear, according to Maritain, that Bergsonian philosophy is incompatible with the Christian creed. Faith in Bergsonian terms is pure inner experience, rather than the assent given by the intelligence to revealed truth. Since reality cannot be expressed in concepts, dogmatic formulas cannot convey knowledge to us. 'The Bergsonian doctrine leads imperceptibly and infallibly to a view of dogmas as transitory and indefinitely improvable expressions of a certain religious feeling which itself is in evolution. If there is no eternal truth and if axioms evolve, why should dogmas not evolve as well?' (*La Philosophie bergsonienne*, p. 167).

Bergsonism, briefly, means the destruction of both faith and reason; it denies a God who could be reached by intellectual efforts, it denies creation *ex nihilo* and the real difference between God and the world; it denies free will and the substantial unity of the human soul; it cannot be reconciled with the idea of incarnation (since personality is defined by change), with the Catholic concept of the Eucharist (since there is no distinction between substance and accident), or with the Revelation (since personal experience is all that counts in religious matters). Maritain sums up his strictures in a magnificent statement reminiscent of Savonarola: 'A poor peasant who believes that God created Heaven and Earth and who believes in the Holy Sacrament of the Altar knows more about truth, Being and substance, than Plotinus, Spinoza and the whole of Bergsonism' (ibid., p. 306).

Maritain's criticism is cogent in that he convincingly demonstrates the incompatibility of Bergson's philosophy with Thomist tenets, and indeed with the Catholic creed as interpreted officially by the Church. Why it is St Thomas, rather than Bergson, who is the possessor of truth, is a different dispute. Maritain clearly believes that the world becomes intelligible when seen through the Aristotelian-Thomist conceptual network; Bergson believed the same about the categories he worked out for himself.

Bergson and modernism

Maritain's arguments are also convincing when he shows the affinity of Bergsonism with the tendencies of Catholic modernism. In the preface to the second edition of 1926, he wrote that his book had been published in an atmosphere of modernism. 'This was a period when many young priests spoke of nothing but Becoming, Immanence, the evolutionary transformation of the expressions of faith, the refraction of the Ineffable through dogmatic formulas that were always provisional and faulty, the ill effects of all abstract knowledge, the impotence of "conceptual" reason in ascertaining the higher truth of the natural order, the idolatrous, superstitious (and above all obsolete) character of the principle of contradiction' (ibid., p. xiv).

There is no doubt that while both emerged and developed independently of one another, Bergsonian philosophy converged with the new trends in Catholicism. Edouard Le Roy, one of the most prominent writers of the modernist movement (and Bergson's future successor in the Académie française) was at the same time the most ardent propagator of the Bergsonian doctrine and his book on the 'New Philosophy' was considered the best initiation into its intricacies.

At the beginning of the twentieth century the modernist movement was widespread among the Catholic intelligentsia of Europe. It tried to modernize both the teaching of the Church and its system of authority in a spirit that conformed to the leading trends of the age. The modernists questioned the authority of the Church in biblical scholarship and demanded that exegetical work be ruled only by the normal criteria of historical research; and they also – especially Alfred Loisy – applied their criticism to various important points in the Gospels which were, in their view, merely expressions of faith of early Christian communities and not infallible and divinely inspired records, immune to errors. They altered the very meaning of revelation and of dogma, arguing that revelation proper is the enlightenment of the individual consciousness by God, rather than a well-defined text supposedly dictated by God, and that the dogmas of the Church, rather than being immutable truth, were provisional and changeable forms in which Christians express their faith according to historical circumstances; the meaning of dogmas is practical rather than cognitive. They made a distinction between the Christ of faith and

Christ the historical figure, and questioned the belief that
he was God's son in a literal sense; the meaning of his
death, as taught by the Church, had been elaborated by St
Paul. They spoke of the evolution both of dogmas and of
sacraments and interpreted the latter as a way for
Christians to become aware of Jesus Christ's presence,
rather than as acts by which supernatural gifts are handed
to the recipients. The modernist view of the constitution
of the Church, including its hierarchical order, and the
Pope's supreme authority, was that they were a result of
historical development, rather than an immutable order
established by Christ. At the same time, Le Roy considered
science a symbolic codification of experience, rather than
truth in the usual sense. Briefly, their interpretation of faith
was subjectivist and historicist; it included the outright
denial of an intellectual way to God, whether by
metaphysical speculation or by historical study. The
modernists considered themselves Christians, certainly,
but by interpreting faith in an anti-scholastic and anti-
Tridentine manner they in fact robbed the Church of all
intellectual instruments of education and they could not
have avoided the stigma of heresy. Sixty-five erroneous
statements by modernists were anathemized by the Holy
Office in July 1907 and two months later the famous
encyclical *Pascendi dominici gregis* by Pius X confirmed
the condemnation; the anti-modernist oath became
obligatory for all priests (it was abolished only by the second
Vatican Council in the early 1960s) and the campaign
against heresy became the main preoccupation of Catholic
intellectuals and indeed of the Church.

Ultimately, the role of Bergson's philosophy in the
Catholic world was ambiguous. On the one hand his books
neutralized, as it were, the materialist impact of science
and demonstrated that recent scientific discoveries –

especially in neurophysiology and the theory of evolution – by no means conflicted with the concept of the immateriality of consciousness and with the idea of God's presence in the universe. Maritain himself was ready to admit that this philosophy helped many people to rediscover God and to abandon atheism. On the other hand Bergson's conceptual apparatus was clearly incompatible with the way the Church interpreted its creed, and the expansion of his ideas reinforced the dangerous heresy. If a final balance can be found at all, it is up to the Church to find it.

Bergson's personal evolution brought him closer and closer to the Catholic faith. Alfred Loisy, after his excommunication, moved further and further away from the Church even though, according to the testimony of Jean Guitton in his book on Bergson, he never renounced his belief in God, and regarded pantheism as an absurdity. In 1934 Loisy published a book with a detailed criticism of Bergson's *Two Sources*, which he called a theogonic poem. He criticized the very restrictive concept of mysticism which in his view was a general and widespread feeling of the presence of spirit and love in the universe. He believed it was impossible to make a sharp dichotomy between 'static' and 'dynamic' religion: each form of religiosity in fact displays both these aspects. And it was unacceptable to him to see Christianity as an absolute beginning. There is no distinction of essence between static and dynamic religion, just as there is none between closed and universal morality or between magic and religion: they coexist, or can be seen as stages of the same spiritual development of mankind.

Followers?

Was there a 'Bergsonism' apart from Bergson himself?

Unlike his contemporary Husserl, Bergson has not left any 'school' which would develop his ideas; he had admirers, propagators, defenders, but no disciples or intellectual successors in the proper sense. Bergson's philosophy was perhaps too impregnated with his unique literary style and rhetorical devices, too personal and expressionistic. It is perhaps an exaggeration to say, with Maritain, that only ideas, not emotions and sympathies, can be communicated: after all, there have been schools of painting and even of poetry. Bergson, however, offered no applicable 'method' apart from his own results; he inspired other people, but left them no ready-made instrument for further research. The impact of his work was wide-reaching and long-lasting, but it was a continuation of particular ideas picked out of the interconnected whole rather than a development of a 'system'. Whitehead's metaphysics, with its attempts to reconcile continuity with novelty, certainly owe much to Bergson's inspiration. It has often been pointed out that Teilhard de Chardin's effort to produce an evolutionary cosmology in which God appears both as the source of initial energy and the ultimate point of convergence, was a new elaboration of Bergson's metaphysics. The German antirationalist *Lebensphilosophie*, opposing creative 'life' to immobilizing 'spirit', took up a number of Bergsonian tenets. Georges Sorel employed Bergson's categories in his political philosophy to combat Marxist historical determinism and to preach a way of thinking which revindicated the unique, the singular, and the contingent, and swept aside intellectualist utopianism and naïve attempts to deduce political programmes from the rationalist description of human nature. His scorn for the theorists of the Second International and his admiration for 'voluntarist' politics, embodied in Bolshevism and Fascism, were expressed in Bergsonian terms.

Bergson

French Existentialist philosophy was also Bergson's heir, usually without acknowledging the debt. The generation of Sartre and Merleau-Ponty was, of course, well acquainted with Bergson's work. None of them was 'Bergsonian' in a recognizable sense, but none of their ideas was conceivable without Bergson's legacy. That human existence is ultimately identical with the consciousness of existence is a Bergsonian tenet which was taken over by Sartre within a radically different metaphysics; in Bergson's philosophy this identity is related to his belief that the whole is of the same nature as the self, whereas Sartre's analysis of consciousness supports his theory of an unbridgeable gap between the self-reflecting being and the world in itself. Both Sartre's refusal to admit any 'substantiality' of the self and his description of time as an act of consciousness are of Bergsonian origin. So too is his nominalism, his denial of the Aristotelian distinction between potentiality and actuality and the recognition that in human existence everything is *in actu*.

This is by no means a complete description; but the way Bergson's thought acted upon European intellectual life showed no clear pattern. Today one would find hardly a single, fully-fledged 'Bergsonian', but few contemporary philosophers could boast of having been entirely beyond Bergson's direct or indirect field of influence. No matter how infrequently he is quoted or referred to, Bergson's presence has not been eradicated from our civilization; once he appeared, philosophical life could never be the same again. It is perhaps impossible to say what exactly has 'remained' of his legacy in the form of particular 'statements'. But it certainly has much to do with the present shaky position of the rationalist creed. Whether we should see this outcome as beneficial or disastrous is a matter of choice.

Summary

It has been pointed out by some critics – in particular by Maritain and Hans Ugo von Balthasar – that in Bergson's writings there are two philosophies incompatible with each other. I believe this remark to be true, even though I would describe these two 'systems' somewhat differently than other commentators.

Briefly speaking, there is on the one hand, the Bergson-Cartesian (or semi-Cartesian) who starts with a version of the *cogito*. He identifies reality with time, and time is necessarily private (only the present is real and the present is related to consciousness); human intelligence, being an organ of the body, is incapable of delivering truths, and our internal time experience is incapable of being expressed. On both sides, cognitive access to matter is blocked. In real experience the uniqueness of time is revealed and the nature of consciousness is never-ending free creativity; we are creative in every act, however trivial. On the other hand there is the Bergson-cosmologist. His starting-point is life contrasted with matter and soul contrasted with brain. He develops not only a cosmogony, but a kind of theogony as well. Life and consciousness appear to the divine effort of creation as its most sublime products. Consciousness is imprisoned in the body, freedom and creativity are by no means its permanent and natural ways of being: they appear infrequently, in contrast to God's creativity, which never ceases to operate. People who transcend the limits of closed society and of static religion derive their energy from the divine *élan*.

In the first version, consciousness is a continuous self-creation *ex nihilo*; in the second, the original direction of the entire process of evolution – though not its details – is divinely inspired. The first version is a neo-Romantic, pagan song in praise of unlimited human creativity, the second is an attempt to assimilate modern science into the modernist-Christian philosophy. The first is Existentialist, the second pantheistic.

These two versions cannot be distinguished according to chronological criteria; they interfere with each other throughout Bergson's work and they tear asunder the philosophical construction. But it would be fair to say that the first version is much more strongly present in the *Essay* and *Introduction to Metaphysics*; the second clearly gains the upper hand in Bergson's later development.

The split was to be naturally revealed, as is always the case with influential philosophers, in the two different kinds of impact that his philosophy had in European culture. The Cartesian aspects were inherited in part by Existentialist philosophers, none of whom could swallow the optimistic and pantheistic cosmology; the latter was taken up and developed by Teilhard de Chardin.

The two versions of Bergsonism collide with each other. One cannot be Descartes and Schelling simultaneously. This collision, however, is not a case of trivial inconsistency. It reveals one of the most painful spots in modern philosophy and its persistent temptation. To find a consistent language which would embrace both the *cogito* and the cosmos is probably impossible; once we start with one we do not reach the other. If we try to run on the same track from both ends, we provoke collision. We may view Bergson's incoherence in a Hegelian manner by tracing it back to the single primordial intuition which split in the process of development into two incongruent parts. At both ends – existential and cosmological – Bergson tried to assert the uniqueness and the autonomous ontological status of human personal existence. Starting with inner experience he discovered consciousness as an absolute creator and he made time its property; then he asserted it as a work of the divine artist. To have it both ways within the same discourse proved to be impossible.

Glossary of names

Avenarius, Richard (1843–96): German philosopher and professor in Zurich. His version of empiricism was aimed at the elimination of all metaphysical questions in favour of pure experience. Though his *Kritik der reinen Erfahrung* (1888–90) makes immensely difficult reading, he was a very influential thinker before the First World War. Hardly anybody reads him any more.

Binet, Alfred (1857–1911): French experimental psychologist, the inventor of a method of measuring the intellectual skills of children, and one of the main figures of the associationist school.

Borel, Émile (1871–1956): eminent French mathematician and politician, professor at the Sorbonne and the École Normale; he criticized Bergson's theory of 'geometrical intelligence'.

Eimer, Theodor (1843–98), German theorist of evolution in terms of 'orthogenesis'; he argued that although a kind of immanent principle of direction, guiding the evolutionary process, has to be admitted, its teleological explanations must be rejected.

Eleatics: a name given to the philosophical school centred in Elea in the fifth century BC. Parmenides and Zeno were its main figures. The central theme of the school was the unity and immutability of Being and the unreality of change and movement.

Mach, Ernst (1838–1916): Austrian physicist and philosopher, and professor in Prague and Vienna. His radically empiricist doctrine did away with the problem of a bridge between the world in itself and its perception, reduced reality to ontologically neutral 'elements', and the validity of scientific theories to their predictive power. Main philosophical works are *Die Analyse der Empfindungen* (1906), and *Erkenntnis and Irrtum* (1905).

Marcel, Gabriel (1889–1973): French philosopher and writer; converted to Catholicism, he became the main proponent of so-called Christian Existentialism; his works include *Être et avoir* (1935) and *Le Mystère de l'être* (1951).

Nicholas of Cusa (Cusanus) (1401–64): one of the greatest minds of the late Middle Ages, mathematician, philosopher, Church reformer, and (from 1448) cardinal; author of *De docta ignorantia*. His philosophy shows a strong pantheistic leaning and stresses the impossibility of employing the principle of contradiction when infinite entities – God in particular – are spoken of.

Renan, Ernest (1823–92): French historian, linguist, and philosopher, the author of the famous and sceptical *Vie de Jésus* (1863). His rationalist, secularist, anti-metaphysical approach to knowledge and his belief in progress, of which the development of mind is the main vehicle, made an enormous impact on French intellectual life in the second half of the nineteenth century.

Sorel, Georges (1847–1922): French political writer, chief ideologist of syndicalism, author of *Les Illusions du progrès* (1908) and *Réflexions sur la violence* (1908). Influenced by Marxism to some extent, he rejected all deterministic interpretations of history and employed the Bergsonian concept of creativity as an instrument both of historical analysis and political projections.

Taine, Hippolyte (1828–93): French historian, art critic, and philosopher, author of the *Histoire de la littérature anglaise* (1863–4) and *Philosophie de l'art* (1865). Although strongly influenced by Spinoza and Hegelianism, he was one of the most active proponents of the positivist spirit in France, which incorporated a rigid determinism, psychophysical parallelism, and a mechanistic interpretation of mental phenomena.

Teilhard de Chardin, Pierre (1881–1955): French Christian philosopher, paleoanthropologist, and Jesuit. His philosophical works (*Le Phénomène humain*, 1955, and *Le Milieu divin*, 1957) were published posthumously as a result of ecclesiastical censorship and became enormously popular in the late fifties and sixties. He elaborated a theory of cosmic evolution and argued that an evolutionary approach, far from being incompatible with Christian wisdom, is in fact its best expression. His philosophy was often seen as pantheistic, rather than orthodox Christian.

Further reading

Works by Bergson

The standard edition of Bergson is *Oeuvres*, Presses Universitaires de France (1970), pp. xxx + 1682. It includes all Bergson's major works: *Essai sur les données immédiates de la conscience, Matière et mémoire, Le Rire, L'Évolution créatrice, L'Énergie spirituelle, Les Deux Sources de la morale et de la religion*, and *La Pensée et le mouvant*, as well as critical apparatus and notes. This volume reproduces the pagination of the original volumes and it is the pagination followed in the present book. There are many editions of individual works.

A number of minor texts, not included in *Oeuvres*, were published in three volumes as *Écrits et paroles*, Presses Universitaires de France (1957–9). These volumes include various speeches, book reviews, polemics, letters, and reports; in accordance with Bergson's wishes, only the texts published in his lifetime are reprinted.

The texts of *Écrits et paroles* are reproduced with substantial additions in *Mélanges*, Presses Universitaires de France (1972), pp. xxiii + 1692. This volume includes the French translation of Bergson's doctoral thesis (*L'Idée de lieu chez Aristote*; the first French version appeared in *Études bergsoniennes*, vol. 2, 1949), *Durée et simultanéité*, and a number of texts omitted by the editors of *Écrits et paroles*.

Bergson

English translations

Time and Free Will. An Essay on the Immediate Data of Consciousness, tr. F. L. Pogson (1910; 6th ed, 1950)

Matter and Memory, tr. N. M. Paul and W. Scott Palmer (1911)

Laughter. An Essay on the Meaning of the Comic, tr. C. Brereton and F. Rothwell (1911)

Creative Evolution, tr. A. Mitchell (1911)

Mind-Energy, tr. H. W. Carr (1920)

An Introduction to Metaphysics, tr. T. E. Hulme (1912 and 1949)

The Two Sources of Morality and Religion, tr. R. A. Andre and C. Brereton (1935)

The Creative Mind, tr. M. L. Andison (1946)

Works on Bergson

As Bergson's philosophy enjoyed its greatest popularity after the publication of *Creative Evolution* (1907) and was still fairly influential after the First World War and in the 1920s, it is not surprising that many important works – analytical and critical – on Bergson had appeared before the publication of his last major work, *Two Sources of Morality and Religion.* Among those early works, E. Le Roy's *Une Philosophie nouvelle, Henri Bergson* (1912; English translation 1913) was perhaps the most widely read as an enthusiastic introduction. Hostile criticism from the rationalist viewpoint includes two books by Julien Benda: *Le Bergsonisme ou une philosophie de la mobilité* (1912) and *Une Philosophie pathétique* (1913), as well as Bertrand Russell's *The Philosophy of Bergson* (1914). Among

Further reading

numerous Thomist critics the most important are: Jacques Maritain, *La Philosophie bergsonienne* (1913, 3rd ed. 1948); J. de Tonquédec, *Dieu dans l'évolution créatrice* (1912); and A. D. Sertillanges, *Henri Bergson et le catholicisme* (1941); the latter's strictures are less intransigeant and leave more room for an eventual reconciliation of Bergson's pantheist doctrine with the Christian tradition. Among authors who show a rather sympathetic approach to the 'new philosophy' before 1932, J. Chevalier, *Henri Bergson* (1926, English translation 1928), W. Carr, *Henri Bergson, The Philosophy of Change*, (1919), and A. Thibaudet, *Le Bergsonisme* (2 vols, 1926) should be mentioned. A. Loisy's *Y a-t-il deux sources de la religion et de la morale?* (1934) is specifically devoted to a critical analysis of Bergson's last work; it is not a criticism of Catholicism, but rather an attack in terms of the history of religion.

Later works which deal with all main aspects of Bergson's philosophy include M. Barlov's *Henri Bergson* (1966), a good general introduction of popular character and, above all, Vladimir Jankelevitch's *Henri Bergson* (1959), a somewhat difficult but elegant work, certainly one of the best analyses of Bergsonian philosophy. An illuminating discussion of major issues in Bergson's philosophy is to be found in Barbara Skarga's *Czas i trwanie* (Time and Duration), 1982 – in Polish, alas. *Le Bergsonisme* (1968), by G. Deleuze, makes interesting but difficult reading: it attempts to present the entire doctrine in terms of the concepts of difference and differentiation. Various aspects of Bergsonism are discussed in a collection of essays edited shortly after Bergson's death by A. Beguin and P. Thevenaz: *Henri Bergson. Essais et témoignages* (1943); some of the essays read rather like obituaries but others offer interesting analytical efforts. The contributors include Paul Valéry, Gabriel Marcel, Jacques Chevalier,

Gaston Berger, and Sertillanges. Other collective works include T. Hanna (ed.), *The Bergsonian Heritage* (1962) and the journal *Les Études bergsoniennes*, vols I–XI (1949–74). Religious meaning in Bergson's philosophy is discussed in a number of works including L. Adolphe, *La philosophie religieuse de Bergson* (1946) and H. Gouhier, *Bergson et le Christ des Évangiles* (1961). The Neoplatonic aspects of this philosophy are analysed in R. M. Mossé-Bastide, *Bergson et Plotin* (1960); the same published *Bergson éducateur* (1955), with a full bibliography. A separate study of Bergson's influence on Teilhard de Chardin was published by M. Barthélemy-Madaule, *Bergson et Teilhard de Chardin* (1963). His importance in French literature is depicted in an Oxford doctoral thesis, A. E. Pilkington, *Bergson and his influence* (1976), a solid and well-informed account of what Proust, Valéry, and Charles Péguy respectively took over or failed to take over from Bergson. J. Guitton's book *La vocation de Bergson* (1960) includes a number of biographical details not given in other sources and follows the development of religious feelings and ideas in Bergson's life.

Index

Index